The International Law Association Helsinki Rules

International Water Law

Volumes published in this Brill Research Perspective are listed at *brill.com/rpwl*

The International Law Association Helsinki Rules

Contribution to International Water Law

By

Slavko Bogdanović

BRILL

LEIDEN | BOSTON

This paperback book edition is simultaneously published as Volume 3(4) 2018 in *International Water Law*, DOI:10.1163/23529369-12340012.

Library of Congress Control Number: 2018968193

Typeface for the Latin, Greek, and Cyrillic scripts: "Brill". See and download: brill.com/brill-typeface.

ISBN 978-90-04-39547-3 (paperback)
ISBN 978-90-04-39548-0 (e-book)

This book is printed on acid-free paper and produced in a sustainable manner.

Contents

The International Law Association Helsinki Rules

Contribution to International Water Law

Slavko Bogdanović
Member, International Law Association
nsslavko@gmail.com

Abstract

Although the International Law Association (ILA) was established in 1873, it only turned its attention to the internationally shared water resources in 1954, when its study of the applicable principles and rules of international law thereon began. The first ILA committee assigned to this task was the Rivers Committee, which, after a decade of intensive study and through several resolutions and statements, arrived unanimously at a set of articles reflecting customary international law, known as The Helsinki Rules on the Uses of the Waters of International Rivers.

The Helsinki Rules approved at the ILA Helsinki Conference in 1966 were soon widely accepted across the globe as a non-binding authoritative source of international water law. This monograph traces the work of ILA leading to the approval of the Helsinki Rules, analyses the Rules, and identifies their influence on, and contribution to the evolution of international water law.

Keywords

equitable and reasonable utilization – Helsinki Rules – International Law Association – Rivers Committee – UN Watercourses Convention

•••

 | DOI:10.1163/9789004395480_002

> All good laws, national and international, must be the fruit of experience.
> H. A. SMITH (1931)

Introduction

August 2016 was the fiftieth anniversary of the resolution of the International Law Association (ILA), issued at the end of its biennial conference in Helsinki in 1966, where the ILA approved a set of principles and rules governing the use and protection of the waters of international drainage basins. This set of articles, the Helsinki Rules on the Uses of the Waters of International Rivers, known under the abbreviated title Helsinki Rules, soon became widely known and accepted by the international community as a source of general rules of international law on the use and protection of the waters of shared drainage basins, applicable in case of absence of a treaty or binding custom. In the following years, the Helsinki Rules became an inspiration for building up relations between states sharing the same freshwaters either through the signing of water treaties, or as a basis for resolution of water disputes.

This half a century anniversary seems to have gone largely unnoticed in the water law professional community. The reasons for that silence might be the result of developments in contemporary international water law, particularly the entry into force and effect of the United Nations Convention on the Law of Non-navigational Uses of International Watercourses (UN Watercourses Convention). However, any attempt to identify such reasons and to try to explain their effects on contemporary perceptions of the Helsinki Rules might be premature. Such efforts might offer no more than a speculative view, which would hardly provide satisfactory answers. The hypothetical question of whether and why, if it is the case, the Helsinki Rules are sinking into the oblivion, could hardly be answered in that way. Therefore, a different approach is required.

In the view of this author, it is beneficial to highlight the historical features of the international context in which the Helsinki Rules evolved, and to try thereafter to understand what their role was, and still is, in the evolution and practical implementation of international water law. In other words, it is beneficial to attempt to position the Helsinki Rules in a timeline reflecting the gradual development and increase in the number of rules capable of securing peaceful settlement of actual or potential controversies between states regarding the use of their shared freshwaters. Such insight will provide a basis for a more constructive assessment of the significance and role of the Helsinki Rules in contemporary international water law.

When starting such an analysis, the contextual timeline might and should be determined as the period that begins with clearly defined broader circumstances of an economic, technical/scientific, legal, developmental, political, and policy character. This would establish an identifiable impetus for certain research and study that will lead towards a contextual understanding of the emergence of the concepts and rules in the Helsinki Rules. The period relevant comprises a span of twelve years of the ILA work (1954–1966) and a review of the period since the ILA was established in 1873. For insight into the influence of the Helsinki Rules, on both the subsequent work of the ILA and further development, codification, and practical implementation of international water law, the timeline spans the period from their approval until today.

The way and method of work concerning the use of the waters of international rivers,[1] initiated by the ILA in 1954, led to a very scrutinized formulation and approval of the Helsinki Rules on the Uses of the Waters of International Rivers (Helsinki Rules) twelve years later (1966),[2] and to the development of a number of specific supplementary and complementary rules and recommendations thereafter (during the period 1966–2000). In 2000, all the ILA rules were compiled into one document, the *Campione Consolidation of the ILA Rules on International Water Resources* (Campione Consolidation). Between 2000 and 2004, the ILA concentrated on the development of the Berlin Rules, which was basically an attempt to revise the entire earlier ILA work in the field of international water law, and to progressively develop that branch of law.[3]

1 The term 'international river' (as opposed to the term 'national river', denominating a 'waterway' in a 'river system' under the exclusive sovereignty and ownership of only one state) has replaced the earlier terms 'common river' and 'conventional river'. *See* P. Sevette, 'Legal Aspects of Hydro-Electric Development of Rivers and Lakes of Common Interest', *UNECE Committee on Electric Power*, UN Doc. No. E/ECE/136, E/ECE/EP/98 Rev. 1, Geneva (1952), at 5–6. Later, other terms denominating the same or slightly different concepts came into use: 'international watercourses', 'shared watercourses', and most recently, 'transboundary watercourses/lakes'. The scope of the concept basically comprises freshwaters marking a boundary between states or being intersected by a state boundary.

2 Professor Friedrich J. Barber (Institute für Völkerrecht der Ludwig-Maximilians Universität of Munich, Germany) described the set of proposed articles as representing 'a delicate balance between widely divergent views', which meant any attempt to change them 'would tend to undermine the compromise, would reopen all problems' and destroy the work done by the Rivers Committee over the last twelve years. ILA, *Report of the 52nd Conference* (Helsinki, 1966), at 462.

3 The revision was undertaken for three reasons:
- None of the most disputed shared freshwaters are covered by an agreement among all the interested states;

Highlighting the details of the work in the half-century-long initial period, when the ILA entered the field and endeavoured to fulfil its constitutional objective,[4] will provide a clearer picture of the atmosphere and priority topics in this field of international law, and of the professional context in which the Helsinki Rules were developed. Important facets of the methodology that the ILA applied will also be highlighted.

The ILA deployed three of its committees to work on the international law of shared water resources. The first, the Committee on the Uses of the Waters of International Rivers (the Rivers Committee) (1954–1966), was assigned 'to study the various legal, economic and technical aspects of rights and obligations between states as to the inland waters, [...] with the purpose of elaborating practical recommendations for international arrangements'.[5] The Rivers Committee submitted six reports to the biennial ILA conferences[6] and produced four documents, leading eventually to the approval of a widely accepted set of principles and rules of international law applicable on the waters of shared drainage basins, namely, the Helsinki Rules. The ILA approved the following documents:

- A Statement of Principles Upon Which to Study Further the Development of Rules of International Law with Respect to International Rivers (Dubrovnik, 1956);
- Heads of Unanimous Agreement; Agreed Principles of International Law; Agreed Recommendations (New York, 1958);

- The process of ratification of the Convention on the Law of Non-navigational Uses of International Watercourses (UN Watercourses Convention) has been slow and there are questions as to whether the Convention always correctly states the law;
- Progressive development of the law is needed to cope with emerging problems of international or global water management. 'The Berlin Rules set about to provide a clear, cogent, and coherent statement of the customary international law', applicable at the waters of international drainage basins and to the all waters within a state to the extent of applicability of customary international law to such waters. *See* ILA, *Report of the 71st Conference* (Berlin, 2004), at 338.

4 *See infra* note 21 and accompanying text.

5 'Resolution (5) Inland Water Rights', ILA, *Report of the 46th Conference* (Edinburgh, 1954), at vii.

6 Reports were submitted to the following ILA conferences: 47th (Dubrovnik, 1956), 48th (New York, 1958), 49th (Hamburg, 1960), 50th (Brussels, 1962), 51st (Tokyo, 1964), and 52nd (Helsinki, 1966). Professor Clyde Eagleton (New York University School of Law) was the Chairman and Rapporteur of the Rivers Committee until his death in January 1958; Professor Arnold Knauth (NY University School of Law) succeeded him until October 1960. Professor Cecil J. Olmstead (NY University School of Law) took over the Chairmanship of the Committee in October 1960 following the death of Knauth that month.

- Hamburg Recommendations on the Procedure Concerning Non-navigational Uses (Hamburg, 1960);
- Hamburg Recommendations on Pollution Control Commissions (Hamburg, 1960);
- Helsinki Rules on the Uses of the Waters of International Rivers (Helsinki, 1966).

This monograph will focus on a detailed elaboration and analysis of the work of the first ILA Committee, the Rivers Committee, and the contents and status of its outputs. The results of the work of two later committees[7] are outside the scope of this study because they were struck after the Helsinki Rules were adopted. However, parts of their outputs are considered here when they directly relate to improving and up-grading provisions of the Helsinki Rules.[8]

It should be expected that contextualization of the Helsinki Rules during the period of development would provide only a partial picture on their significance and their role in developing international water law. An answer to the question as to why this is so can be seen in the fact that, after adoption of the Helsinki Rules, the ILA continued its work on identifying and developing the rules of international water law. During this period (1966–2000), the Helsinki Rules were up-dated and certain details were revised, identified gaps were filled in, and, finally, the approved rules were consolidated. The Helsinki Rules (1966) are the backbone of the Campione Consolidation (2000). Therefore, for a full understanding of the meaning and importance of the Helsinki Rules and insight into the unprecedented professional journey of one of world's oldest organizations of international lawyers (ILA), further contextual positioning of the Helsinki Rules during the period 1966–2004 is necessary.

This monograph starts with a review of the first period of the ILA efforts, the activities and the outcome of the Rivers Committee work, and analyses the documents drafted by the Committee. Under the strong supervision and precise guidelines of the managing bodies of the ILA, this work led step-by-step to the approval of the Helsinki Rules at the 1996 ILA Conference. This is followed by a discussion about the Helsinki Conference and its resolution, and then a

7 The ILA later struck two other water law committees: The Committee on International Water Resources Law (Manner's Committee, 1966–1986), chaired by Judge Eero Manner (Finland), and the Water Resources Committee (1990–2004), chaired (1990–2000) by Professor Charles Bourne (University of British Columbia, Vancouver) and (2000–2004) by Professor Gerhard Loibl (Diplomatic Academy, Wien, Austria).

8 For a discussion of the work of the ILA, *see* E. J. Manner & V. M. Mestälampi (eds.), *The Work of the International Law Association on the Law of International Water Resources* (Helsinki: Finnish Branch of ILA, 1988); C. Bourne, *'The International Law Association's Contribution to International Water Resources Law'*, 36 Natural Resources Journal (1996), 155–216.

detailed analysis of each chapter of the Helsinki Rules. The concluding part of this monograph highlights the global acceptance and wide influence exerted by the Helsinki Rules on shared watercourses issues and related disputes, in particular the UN Watercourses Convention.

Part 1: The Birth of the International Law Association

1.1 *The Inception and Mission of the International Law Association*

The Association for the Reform and Codification of the Law of Nations was founded at a conference held on 19 October 1873 in Brussels following an inception idea by several distinguished American jurists that a code of international law should be prepared by an international association. Elihu Burritt, a diplomat, philanthropist and social activist, Reverend Dr. James B. Miles, Secretary of American Peace Society, and the Honourable David Dudley Field, a member of the New York Bar and draftsman of the Civil Code of the State of New York[9] were convinced that the code must precede any general resort to international arbitration. For them, the lack of such code hindered the general substitution of Arbitration for War. Supported by Field, Miles went to Europe 'to invite adhesion' to the idea. At the same time, a number of leading European lawyers had been considering forming an association 'with the object of establishing on a scientific basis the foundations of international jurisprudence'. At a meeting in Ghent on 8 September 1873, the Institute of International Law (IIL) was formed as a learned society.[10] At that meeting, a 'deputation of eight members' was appointed to attend the October conference in Brussels that established the Association for the Reform and Codification of the Law of Nations. It became clear that the existence of a code of international law was not 'an essential prerequisite to the judicial settlement of international disputes'. The Association, which changed its name to the International Law Association at its 1885 Brussels conference, focussed its attention on other issues, 'aiming at uniformity of law and practice' through 'improvements rather than re-stated existing law'.[11]

The IIL and the ILA differ substantially from each other in the nature of their institutional profile, but not in their objectives and purpose. The IIL has

9 Field was also one of the eleven founders of the Institut de Droit International (IDI)/ Institute of International Law (IIL).

10 Statutes of the Institute of International Law, Ghent, 10 September 1873, Article 1 (1). http://www.idi-iil.org/app/uploads/2017/06/Statutes-of-the-Institute-of-International-Law.pdf.

11 *See* ILA, *Report of the 46th Conference* (Edinburg, 1954), at x–xi.

been defined as an 'exclusively learned society, without any official nature' with the purpose of promoting the progress of international law.[12] The means of promotion were defined, *inter alia*, as striving to formulate general principles that correspond to the legal conscience of the civilized world, lending its cooperation in any serious endeavour for the gradual and progressive codification of international law, contributing to the maintenance of peace or to the observance of the laws of war, and studying difficulties that may arise in the interpretation or application of the law, and issuing reasoned legal opinions in doubtful or controversial cases. The total number of members and associates of IIL under the age of 80 shall not exceed 132, 'but need not necessarily be equal to that'.[13] The IIL was awarded the Nobel Peace Prize in 1904 for promoting international arbitration and persuading states to accept the rules of law in wartime.[14]

The ILA has a legal status of an international non-governmental organization (NGO). In contrast to the IIL, the ILA consists of persons and organizations, elected by branches and by the Executive Council, and honorary members, elected by a Council. Currently, the ILA has over 4,400 members.[15]

Both the IIL and the ILA deal with issues regarding utilization of international rivers. The notable results (i.e., formulated legal provisions in the form of articles) of the IIL concerning international water resources include two resolutions on navigation,[16] a resolution on the pollution of rivers and lakes,[17] and two resolutions regarding utilization of international watercourses/non-maritime waters.[18] At certain times, the two organizations not only shared the same interests, but undertook parallel efforts on specific issues of international water law. Some details about these joint efforts and their results is discussed below in the context of the development of the Helsinki Rules.

1.2 *Entering into* Tera Incognita

Prior to 1954, the ILA had achieved great success in various fields of international law that are beyond the scope of this monograph. However, it should be

12 IIL Statutes, *supra* note 10, art. 1, as revised.

13 *Id.*, art. 3.

14 For details *see* 'Institute of International Law History,' The Nobel Prize.org, Nobel Media AB (2018), https://www.nobelprize.org/prizes/peace/1904/international-law/history/.

15 For more details *see* the new Constitution of the Association, adopted at the 77th Conference (Johannesburg, 2016), http://www.ila-hq.org/images/ILA/docs/constitution_english_adopted_johannesburg_2016.pdf.

16 Heidelberg, 1887; Paris, 1934.

17 Athens, 1979.

18 Madrid, 1911; Salzburg, 1961.

said that the results of its work, in terms of approved resolutions and drafted model rules of law or practice, were considered as having an important influence on legislation in various States. At that time, the reforms foreseen and desired by the ILA were to be implemented by international treaties, national legislation, or business contracts. The ILA Edinburgh Conference Report (1954) stated:

> Now that the United Nations Charter entrusts the General Assembly with promoting the progressive development of international law and its codification,[19] the Association is preparing to play its full part in this task.[20]

According to the ILA Constitution,[21] the objects of the Association include the study, elucidation, and advancement of international public and private law, the study of comparative law, making proposals for the resolution of conflicts of law and for the unification of law, and the furthering international understanding and goodwill. In view of Article 13.1 (a) of the UN Charter and in accordance with the ILA Constitution, as amended at the Copenhagen Conference (1950),[22] the ILA endeavoured to play its full part as regards inland water rights, which was one issue identified at the Edinburgh Conference as deserving deployment of its resources. This is the starting point of the story which follows.

Before this story continues in a chronological order, it seems appropriate to highlight what is probably the first effort to compile an account of international law, including principles, rules, and state practice, applicable on international rivers, prepared by Georges Kaeckenbeeck (United Kingdom) in 1918. This pioneering work was the result of a scholar who 'impressed by the horrors of the present War [World War I], feels however, that the removal of every likely cause of quarrel or dispute is a gain for the cause of peace and a boon for the world.[23] His monograph was compiled materials from

19 Charter of the United Nations, 24 October 1945, art. 13.1 (a).

20 ILA, *Report of the 46th Conference* (Edinburg, 1954), at xii.

21 ILA Constitution, *infra* note 22, art. II.

22 ILA, *Report of the 46th Conference* (Edinburg, 1954), at xviii.

23 G. Kaeckenbeeck, *International Rivers: A Monograph Based on Diplomatic Documents* (London: Sweet and Maxwell, published for the Grotius Society, 1918), at v. In the 'Introductory Note' to this monograph, Professor Henry Goudy noted that the 'bewildering mass of provisions in treaties [...] dealing with international rivers since the beginning of last century [nineteenth] [...] have been subjected to a careful examination and analysis, and [...] placed before the reader in a clear conspectus, and that nothing similar has been attempted before,' at xxv–xxvi.

diplomatic sources 'gathered rather than [...] imposing conclusions without giving premises'. He focussed on navigation, particularly the issues of opening up international rivers to the flags of all nations equally and administrative arrangements between riparian governments for unification of the regime of a river.[24] However, Kaeckenbeeck noted that compiled sources had not generally dealt with the issues connected to the use of international waters for industrial and agricultural purposes, and pointed out that it is

> indispensable to forbid: (1) the injurious pollution of the water, notably by the discharge of industrial residues; (2) such drawing of water, for hydraulic exploitation, [...] as may influence the sources or navigability of the river; (3) the construction of works or weirs which might cause inundation in the territory of a co-riparian; (4) and, generally, all interference which may cause modifications of the actual condition of the waterway, except by the common agreement of all riparians.[25]

Under the current ILA Constitution (2016),[26] the objectives of the ILA are the study, clarification and development of international law, both public and private, and the furtherance of international understanding and respect for international law. Based on that attitude that international law is key to peace, justice and development in a globalized world, its mission statement comprises, in addition to the constitutional objectives defined in 1873, the aims of bringing together all those interested in international law worldwide, which includes those from the legal and mediation practice, the judiciary, academia, business and international, governmental and non-governmental organizations, fostering understanding of international law, and promoting greater respect for and adherence to international law.[27]

Part 2: The Early Years of International Water Law

2.1 *The Period before World War II*

Traditionally, at the beginning of twentieth century, the main interest of states for using 'common rivers' was primarily navigation, which was seen as having

24 *Id.*, at vii.
25 *Id.*, at 181.
26 ILA Constitution, *supra* note 15, art. 3.
27 'International Law Association Mission Statement', ILA, http://www.ila-hq.org/images/ILA/docs/ila_mission_statement_english_french_.pdf.

priority over other uses.[28] However, states sharing waters had increasing needs caused, for example, by industrial development and population growth, *which* meant that other uses had gradually become important, notably development of hydraulic power, irrigation, and flood control projects. The negative effects of diversion of waters of an international river by riparian states for their sole use as well as increased pollution of waters evolved into issues deserving the attention of all riparian states.[29]

In parallel, the international community gradually became interested in the search for the principles and rules of international law applicable in such cases. In addition to academic books dealing with national water law systems, governments and scholars were increasingly interested in the origin and contemporary applicability of the concepts of law developed in Roman Law, medieval feudal law, and the Law of Nature on the use of international rivers. A new field of investigation was opened concerning the practice of states in regulating their bilateral and multilateral relations for their 'common rivers'. The peace and boundary treaties concluded between sovereign states in the period after 1648[30] were of particular interest. Subsequently, the League of

28 Professor Herbert A. Smith (University of London) commented on Fouchille, who pleaded for recognition of an 'universal right of navigation in all navigable rivers in the world' that would give navigation preference. The theoretical basis of such a preference was the opinion that the rivers are extensions of the seas, and therefore subject to the law of sea and to municipal law only in the scope of applicable municipal law to the territorial sea. While uses of water other than navigation are only subject to regulation by municipal law, navigation has preference over all other uses. Smith commented: 'The reasoning is entirely logical, but those of us who cannot accept its premises will naturally find it impossible to agree to its conclusions'. H. A. Smith, *The Economic Uses of International Rivers* (London: P. S. King & Son, 1931), at 137. Moreover, unaffected (in terms of serious injury) navigation on an international waterway has been considered the only restriction on the right of sovereignty when diverting the waters of a navigable river for other purposes, the right of diversion being recognized by international law. Such view was expressed by Mr. William Pugsley, then Canadian Minister of Public Works, before the Canadian House of Commons during the debate on the 1909 Boundary Water Treaty between the United States and Canada. *See* Sevette, *supra* note 1, at 120–121. For more details, *see* C. Bourne, *International Water Law: Selected Writings of Professor Charles Bourne*, ed. by Patricia Wouters (London/The Hague/Boston: Kluwer Law International, 1997), at 294–295.

29 C. Eagleton, *'Diversion of Water in International Rivers: Preliminary Study Outline'*, in ILA, *Report of the 46th Conference* (Edinburg, 1954), at 324–332.

30 The Westphalia peace treaties (Münster and Osnabrück, 1648) set out the co-existence of the sovereign states, which mutually recognized each other as the members of 'a community in public law'. They include the Treaty of Paris (1814); The Final Act of the Congress in Vienna (1815); Treaty of Paris (1856); Treaty of Berlin (1878) and the Conference of Berlin (1884–85); and Treaty of Versailles (with Germany, 1919), of Saint Germaine (with Austria, 1919). Earlier treaties and conferences might also be mentioned, for example, the

Nations and different bodies and agencies of the United Nations and several international organizations dedicated their efforts to investigating and formulating the principles and rules of international law relevant for economic use of international waters.

2.1.1 The Madrid Declaration (1911)

The IIL made the first attempt to identify and formulate a set of rules governing the behaviour of states when using the waters of a watercourse forming the boundary between them and a watercourse traversing their territories for the purposes other than navigation, 'without prejudice to the right of navigation in so far as it is already, or shall be regulated by international law'. The IIL adopted the Declaration on International Regulations regarding the Use of International Watercourses for Purposes Other Than Navigation, also known as the Madrid Declaration (1911).[31] Among the issues tackled, the Declaration stated that no changes may be made by establishments of either state at the point where a watercourse crosses the boundary between them without the consent of the other.[32] The principles set out in the Madrid Declaration were incorporated into the text of treaties developed under the aegis of the League of Nations.[33] The Geneva Convention (1923), particularly the results of the preparatory work, that is, the ideas and guiding principles underlying debates preceding the signing of the Convention, were considered important during the drafting process of the Montevideo Declaration (1933) and, occasionally, in treaty law.[34] The Statute of the Barcelona Convention contains provisions binding each riparian state 'to refrain from all measures likely to prejudice the navigability of the waterway' ensuring that a state cannot refuse

---

Treaty of Fontainebleau (1785), the Treaty of The Hague (1795), the Congress of Radstadt (1797–1798), and the Conference of Ratisborn (1802). For a detailed insight into the relevant diplomatic sources of the time *see* Kaeckenbaeeck, *supra* note 23.

31 The resolution was based on the two reports of the rapporteur Professor Ludvig von Bar (University of Götingen) submitted to the Sixth Commission of the IIL regarding international regulation of international watercourses from the viewpoint of exploitation of their forces and other uses in general. His second report contained the contra-proposals of M. Kaufmann (University of Berlin). IIL, *Annuaire de l'Institut de Droit International, Session de Madrid* (April 1911), at 156–199.

32 The first of the seven defined rules in the Declaration.

33 Convention and Statute on the Regime of Navigable Waterways of International Concern, together with Additional Protocol to the Convention, Barcelona, 20 April 1921 [Barcelona Convention] and Convention of Geneva relating to the Development of Hydraulic Power Affecting More than One State and Protocol of Signature, Geneva, 9 December 1923 [Geneva Convention].

34 For more details *see* Sevette, *supra* note 1, at 47–48.

to carry out works necessary for improving navigability that are requested by another state (which would originate from such interests as maintenance of normal water conditions, irrigation, and use of water power).[35]

The Madrid Declaration was the first institutional attempt of an eminent world organization of international lawyers focussed on codification of the *terra incognita* of the law relating to what was later formulated as 'the legal problems relating to utilization of international rivers' and 'non-navigational uses of international watercourses'. Having that context in mind, it is understandable that the Declaration gave reasons for the critical examination of the principles formulated 'with all due deference.' In his analysis, Smith established that no legal distinction is necessary between boundary (frontier; contiguous) and successive (traversing) rivers. 'If the principle be sound that every river system must be treated as a single physical unit', the interests of two or more states are important, but not 'whether or not the bed of the river coincides with [...] the political frontier.' He also criticized the failure of the Declaration to provide examples of when the consent of a riparian state cannot be reasonably refused at the point where the river crosses the boundary, because 'the duty of giving consent is just as important as the right of withholding it'. Smith found the established right of navigation was 'not entirely clear' in the Declaration, but 'may be pleaded as an insuperable obstacle to any scheme for further development of the river'. From a methodological standpoint, the limited insight into available international treaties during the preparation process of the Madrid Declaration was also noted.[36] In conclusion, Smith stated that

> the resolutions illustrate the dangers of premature attempts at codification, even when undertaken by jurists of the highest distinction [...]. In the light of what we now know [1931], it is clear that the formal incorporation of the proposed rules into the body of positive international law would have proved a serious obstacle to the economic development of river systems[....] [T]he subject is clearly one which is not ripe for codification at present day.[37]

2.1.2 The Barcelona Convention (1921)

The objective of the Barcelona Convention was to achieve a general agreement regarding the principle of freedom of navigation on international waterways.

---

35 Statute of the Barcelona Convention, *supra* note 33, art. 10, paras. 1 and 3 respectively.

36 Smith, *supra* note 28, at 155–157.

37 *Id.*, at 157–158.

When considering its practical value, Smith noted that the Convention did not in general govern 'the Rhine, the Scheldt, the Meuse, the Danube, the Vistula, the Nile, the St. Lawrence, the Congo, the Amazon, the Parana, and many other waterways of international interest', which were already controlled by the other treaties signed by interested states. He specifically pointed out the fact that the Convention had been ratified by those states 'which have not got any international waterways of importance'.[38] The Convention is still in force.[39]

2.1.3 The Geneva Convention (1923)

The Geneva Convention relating to the development of hydraulic power affecting more than one state was approved by the Second General Conference on Freedom of Communication and Transit convened by the League of Nations on 10 November 1923.[40] The Convention, *inter alia*, recognized the right to each state to carry out in its own territory any desirable operation for a reasonable development of hydraulic power, within the limits of international law.[41] If such development might cause serious injury to any other contracting state, the states concerned shall enter into negotiations with the view to concluding an agreement that will be the basis for execution of such works.[42] The Convention was based on the idea of international solidarity and, accordingly, incorporated the principle of the duty to cooperate. Unfortunately, the duty to cooperate was accompanied by the possibility of opposing the development proposal of one state on the basis of 'vital interests' of another riparian state. The Convention has been ratified by several states. However, the Convention has had no practical effect because only two parties to the Convention 'may be called riparian States'.[43] Smith commented:

> It is obvious that this Convention has been drawn in terms which impose no positive international obligations of any kind, and the first article

38 *Id.*, at 192.

39 For an up-dated list of ratifications, *see* United Nations Treaty Collection, https://treaties.un.org/doc/Publication/MTDSG/Volume%20II/LON/PARTII-17.en.pdf.

40 Geneva Convention, *supra* note 33. The Convention entered into force on 30 June 1925. For more details, *see* UN Secretary-General, 'Legal Problems Relating to the Utilization and Use of International Rivers', UN Doc. No. A/5409, 15 April 1963, adopted by the UNGA Resolution 3071 (XXVIII), at 57–60.

41 Geneva Convention, *id.*, arts. 1 and 2.

42 *Id.*, art. 4.

43 For more details, *see* UN Secretary-General Report, *supra* note 40 at 58.

clearly indicates that no attempt has been made to solve the problems which experience has shown to be most difficult.

It will be observed that three of the ratifying States are islands, and none of them have any waterway in common.[44]

2.1.4 The Montevideo Declaration (1933)

The Pan-American Union's[45] Declaration concerning Industrial and Agricultural Use of International Rivers (Montevideo Declaration) was prepared by the Permanent Committee on Codification of Public International Law[46] and adopted at the Seventh Conference of American States[47] and is an authoritative example of the progressive codification of international law.[48] Regarding industrial and agricultural uses, the Montevideo Declaration states that a state has an 'exclusive right to exploit [...] the margin which is under their jurisdiction' of the waters of an international river, with the condition of 'not injuring the equal right due to the neighbouring state over the margin under its jurisdiction'. This was followed by the ban on any alteration that might be injurious to the margin of another state without the consent of the affected state. In cases of repairable damage, the planned work may be executed only after reaching agreement regarding indemnity, reparation, or compensation.[49] The works of industrial and agricultural exploitation performed must not obstruct navigation on a successive river, but instead try to improve it so far as possible.[50] During the preparatory stage, the Permanent Committee concluded that agreement between riparian states is indispensable for utilization of international rivers for industrial and agricultural purposes.[51]

---

44 Smith, *supra* note 28, at 199.

45 The Pan-American Union of American States was formed in 1890 to promote cooperation among the countries of Latin America and the United States.

46 The Committee was appointed by the Government of Brazil, with its seat at Rio de Janeiro (1931).

47 The Declaration was adopted by the Seventh International Conference of American States (Montevideo, 3 December 1933).

48 Pan American Union, *Seventh International Conference of American States, Montevideo, Uruguay, December 3, 1933, Special Handbook for the Use of Delegates*, prepared by L. S. Rowe & G. E. Borges (Baltimore, Maryland: The Sun Book & Job Printing Office, 1933), at 53–56.

49 Declaration Concerning the Industrial and Agricultural Use of International Rivers, Montevideo, 24 December 1933, para. 2.

50 *Id.*, para. 6.

51 'Report of the Permanent Committee on Public International Law of Rio de Janeiro on the general principles which may facilitate regional agreements between adjacent states on the industrial and agricultural use of the waters of international rivers', Rio de Janeiro, 23 July 1932. *See* Sevette, *supra* note 1, at 268–270.

2.2 *Drivers of Change after World War II*

On the initiative of the US President Harry Truman,[52] the UN Economic and Social Council (ECOSOC) decided in March 1947 to organize a scientific conference on resource conservation and utilization. Two years later, the United Nations Educational, Scientific and Cultural Organization (UNESCO) organized the first ever world environmental conference (UNSCCUR).[53] UNSCCUR brought together 'a large and representative group' of over 700 scientists, from 50 countries, who submitted over 500 scientific papers (covering mineral resources, fuel and energy, water, forest, land, wildlife, and fish resources).[54] The Tennessee Valley Authority was identified as the main initiative that highlighted the necessity of viewing the entire integrated river basin when developing all water uses.[55]

The large increase in electric energy consumption in Europe after WW II[56] resulted in the necessity of harnessing the hydropower potential of international rivers. The Committee on Electric Power of the UN Economic Commission for Europe (UNECE) was concerned about complexity of the legal problems and legal difficulties that might impact development of an European policy on electric power. It undertook comprehensive research[57] that resulted in, *inter alia*, the study entitled *Legal Aspects of Hydro-Electric Development of Rivers and Lakes of Common Interest* prepared by Pierre Sevette, Chief of the Power Section of the UNECE Power & Still Division.[58] One of the conclusions

---

52 Set out in a letter to the representative of the United States to the United Nations Economic and Social Council (ECOSOC), UN Doc. No. E/139. 4 September 1946.

53 United Nations Educational, Scientific and Cultural Organization, 'The Scientific Conference on Resource Conservation and Utilization (UNSCCUR)', UN Doc. NS/UNR/1, 10 November 1948, http://unesdoc.unesco.org/images/0015/001547/154751eb.pdf. UNSCCUR was held 17 August–6 September 1949 at Lake Success, New York.

54 *See* ECOSOC, 'Report on the Conference by the Secretary-General', 10th Session, UN Doc. E/1579, 28 December 1949.

55 *See* UNSCCUR, *'The Integrated Development of River Basins', Proceedings of UNSCCUR, 17 August–6 September 1949, Volume 1, Plenary Meetings*, at 387–403. https://archive.org/details/proceedingsoftheo29855mbp/page/n453.

56 *See* UNECE, *'The First Ten Years 1947–1957'*, UN Doc. E/ECE/291 (3 July 1957), at V-1–V-5.

57 Behind this research effort, which was aimed at helping 'governments to find suitable solutions for [...] practical problems', were 'strong indications that the countries of EU [...] are seeking to emerge from an era of international policy based on the idea of rivalry between nations to a new era dominated by the idea of conscious solidarity', which must be the 'basis for replacement of the international law based on rivalry'. Sevette, *supra* note 1, at 2.

58 *Id.* The study was completed in March 1950 and published by UNECE in 1952.

of the study was that the community of interests,[59] equity, and international comity should facilitate the conclusion of agreements between riparian states. Unilateral development of a section of a waterway in the territory of one riparian state is its sovereign right, in so far as such development only causes a slight injury or minor inconvenience that is tolerable in the context of good neighbourly relations. If the result is a serious and lasting injury, prior agreement should be the basis for undertaking such works.[60]

A group of experts examined the Sevette's study and drafted recommendations focussed on hydroelectric development that were adopted by the Committee.[61] It was concluded that a clear distinction between successive and contiguous rivers must be made, that preparation of a general (multilateral) convention would be difficult, and that specific issues could be resolved only by means of agreements between interested states.[62] A distinction between slight and serious and lasting injury was regarded as an important issue that to be addressed in the context of good neighbourly relations and solidarity.[63]

During 1950s, the UNECE Committee on Electric Power adopted two resolutions concerning hydroelectric development on contiguous and successive rivers. In the case of successive rivers, the Committee gave preference to concluding an agreement between the involved states rather than a general convention. The Committee noted that hydroelectric development on rivers or lakes that served as a frontier between two or more states (contiguous) was of 'increasingly great importance for development of European electrical resources and for the satisfaction of the requirements of the European economy'. It called on governments to introduce regulations through treaties with provisions for the same legal treatment of construction of works irrespective of the site chosen. The Committee also considered different aspects of custom/tax exemptions regarding such works, and made certain procedural and technical/legal recommendations regarding the construction works.[64]

---

59 The community of interest of the riparian states of a river traversing or separating their territories was identified as a principle governing international fluvial law/international river law in general in the Permanent Court of International Justice (PCIJ) judgment in the *Case relating to the Territorial Jurisdiction of the International Commission of the River Oder (United Kingdom v. Poland)*, PCIJ Ser. A No. 23 (1929) (*River Oder Case*).

60 *See* Sevette, *supra* note 1, at 210–211.

61 *Id.*, Annex 11, at 301–308.

62 *Id.*

63 *Id.*, at 211–213.

64 Recommendation No. 2 submitted to Governments by the Committee on Electric Power with a view to facilitating the hydro-electric development of contiguous rivers and lakes, 3 October 1951. *See* text in UN Doc. E/ECE/EP/117, available in United Nations Food and Agriculture Organization (FAO), *Some General Conventions, Declarations and Resolutions*

A few years later, the Committee recommended that a state 'proposing to embark within its own territory on projects likely to have serious repercussions on the territory of other states, whether up-stream or downstream' first notify other states as to its intentions. In cases where there were objections, the government was to negotiate with the objecting states with the aim of reaching an agreement 'such as will ensure the most economic development of the river system'.[65]

UNSCCUR led to the adoption of new ECOSOC resolutions. The first resolution noted, *inter alia*,

> the desirability that measures being taken internationally in the general field of water control and utilization should be co-ordinated, and that such co-ordination should be undertaken within the United Nations system.[66]

The UN Secretary-General was requested 'to submit a report to the Council on the work being done by the specialized agencies and other international organizations, whether governmental, semi-governmental or non-governmental in the broad field of water control and utilization'. In his report entitled *International Co-operation on Water Control and Utilization*,[67] the UN Secretary-General observed that '[t]he making of analytical studies by international organizations is limited almost entirely' to the UN and its agencies. The report highlighted legal and administrative aspects identified by the United Nations

---

adopted by Governments, International Legal Institutions and International Organizations, on the Management of International Water Resources, compiled by Dante A. Caponera, Background Paper No. 1/Rev. 1, Legislative Branch (Rome: FAO, 1978), at 141, http://www.fao.org/docrep/012/ak459E/ak459E.pdf.

65 Recommendation No. 4 submitted to Governments by the Committee on Electric Power with a view to promoting the hydro-electric development of successive rivers in Europe, May 1954. *See* 'Legal problems relating to the non-navigational uses of international watercourses. Supplementary Report submitted by the Secretary-General', UN Doc. No. A/CN.4/274, 25 March 1974, reprinted in *Yearbook of the International Law Commission*, 1974, Vol. II, Part Two, at para. 343; *see* also FAO, *supra* note 64, at 143.

66 ECOSOC, Resolution 346 (XII) on International Co-operation on Water Control and Utilization (9 March 1951).

67 Following the request that a report be prepared in consultation with the specialized agencies, in order to obtain information, the Secretary-General sent a circular letter to the specialized UN organizations and to 82 international organizations. The ILA was one of the organizations contacted, but at the outset, the ILA was listed in a group of organizations that 'either reported no pertinent activities or failed to respond'. *See* ECOSOC, '*International Co-operation on Water Control and Utilization, Report of the UN Secretary-General under Council Resolution 346 (XII)*', ECOSOC Doc. E/2205, 25 April 1952.

Food and Agriculture Organization in its report concerning the national water law systems in the United States and Italy and by the UNECE concerning 'legal problems affecting international cooperation for hydroelectric development'.[68] Another resolution followed the report, requesting, *inter alia*, the UN Secretary-General, in consultation with specialized agencies and other organizations,

> to assume responsibility for promotion and co-ordination of international activities concerning water resource development and co-operative action among national authorities and international organizations in order to secure the maximum contribution to economic development through the effective development, control and use of water resources.[69]

The resolution called on the UN Secretary-General to consider suggestions of the Member States, to collaborate with UN agencies, to ask advice of experts and establish inter-agency arrangements for consultations, and to report periodically to the Council on the progress of relevant activities carried out by international organizations.[70]

This call for co-ordination of international activities concerning water control and utilization seems to have had no immediate effects. Therefore, due to the lack of results from this resolution, UN Secretary General Trygve Lie, Andrew Cordier, his executive assistant, and Roy Blough, economist in the Secretariat, which was responsible for implementation of the resolution, announced in the early 1953, that

> [t]he UN would be pleased if someone outside, a non-profit, non-government agency or foundation, would interest itself and undertake activity' aimed at establishing procedures whereby there would be recognized sharing of waters on international streams, and nations would be enabled to determine what water was whose.[71]

68 *Id.*, at 42–43.

69 ECOSOC, Resolution 417 (XIV) on International Co-operation on Water Control and Utilization and on the Development of Arid Land (2 June 1952), para. 1 (a).

70 *Id.*, para. 1.

71 According to Laylin (who referred to the Bulletin on *'International Water Problems'*, 17 (March, 1953) prepared by the Office of Foreign Activities, Bureau of Reclamation, for its administrative use), *'The uses of international rivers'*, Comments submitted to the Committee of American Branch of the ILA on *'First Report of the Committee on the uses of the waters of international rivers'*, 4 May 1956, printed by the ILA for the Dubrovnik Conference (1956), at 19 and 56. *See* The World Bank Group, Archives Public Disclosure Authorized; *Folder: Indus Basin Dispute—International Law Association—Correspondence 01, Folder ID: 1787921*; Dates 5/1/1954–10/31/1958; Fonds: Records of the South Asia Regional

From these initial steps, the interest in the UN on this issue continued throughout the 1950s and 1960s. The outcome of such persistent effort is known and will be briefly commented on below in this monograph, following a brief description and analysis of international water law as it evolved during this period.

Part 3: International Water Law in the 1950s and 1960s

3.1 *The Quest for a Just and Equitable Balancing of the Interests of Riparians*

When the ILA began its journey in the field of the international water law in the early 1950s, there were a considerable number of scholarly books and papers elaborating the law, theories, and principles in that field. It is not possible to provide here more than a brief indication that relevant bibliographies were completed at the time and published under the aegis of UNECE[72] and to note the output of a project implemented by the New York University School of Law.[73] Nonetheless, during this period, the body of international law applicable to use of the international water resources was underdeveloped. The available sources of law[74] were the outcome of efforts of the IIL, an 'exclusively learned society', the League of Nations, and the Pan-American Union.

In an attempt to identify the general principles of international law applicable to watercourses or systems of rivers and lakes (non-maritime waters), which traverse or divide the territory of two or more states, the Inter-American Bar Association adopted the Declaration of Buenos Aires (1957).[75] The Declaration stated that every state has the right to use such waters insofar as such use does not affect adversely the equal right of other states sharing the same waters. The principle of equality of the rights of all states having jurisdiction over such waters in sharing benefits was also declared, accompanied by a

Office (WB IBRD/IDA SAR); Washington, DC, 2012, Digitized: 5 August 2014 [hereinafter World Bank Archives Disclosure Authorized, Folder ID: 1787921].

72 *See* Sevette, *supra* note 1, Annex 14, at 329–333.

73 *See* L. A. Teclaff & E. Teclaff, *'Bibliography on Legal and Related Aspects of the Use and Development of the Waters of International River Basins'*, in A. H. Garretson, R. D. Hayton & C. J. Olmstead (eds.), *The Law of International Drainage Basins* (Dobbs Ferry, NY: Oceana Publications, 1967), at 609–778.

74 Madrid Declaration (1911), Barcelona Convention (1921), Geneva Convention (1923), and Montevideo Declaration (1933).

75 *Principios de derecho que regulan el uso de los ríos internacionales*, adopted unanimously, Buenos Aires, 19 November 1957, text in: Inter-American Bar Association, *Proceedings of the Tenth Conference, Buenos Aires, 14–21 November 1957* (Buenos Aires, 1958), Vol. 1, pp. 246–248, see also FAO, *supra* note 64, at 327–328.

requirement that each state respect the status of existing beneficial uses and enjoy the benefits of future developments according to their respective needs. In cases where is not possible to reach agreement, resort should be made to an international court or an arbitral commission. According to international law, if the flow of such waters provides a particular benefit to the state in whose territory it flows, the benefit may be enjoyed exclusively by that state, but in conformity with the duty to refrain from making changes to the existing regime that might adversely affect the use of one or more states sharing such waters. An agreement with affected state(s) or a decision of an international court or arbitral commission may set the basis for non-application of a duty to refrain.

Treaty law comprised some two hundred international treaties concerning utilization of waters of international rivers, including peace treaties and boundary treaties. In his study, Sevette grouped these instruments into those regulating bilateral relations concerning hydroelectric development of waterways of common interest, bilateral relations concerning general use of waterways of common interest, and multilateral relations concerning general use of waterways of common interest. The Geneva Convention (1923) was grouped alone in a separate category.[76]

During this period, the number of relevant judicial and arbitral decisions concerning the use of waters of international rivers was limited. One of the most often quoted and referred to was the Permanent Court of International Justice (PCIJ) judgement in the *River Oder Case* (1929).[77] In the search for the 'possibility of fulfilling the requirements of justice' concerning the issue of navigation, in light of the fact that a river traverses or separates the territories of more than one state, the Court did not find the right of passage to the sea in favour of upstream countries, but in the community of interest of riparian states. The expression of the principle of community of interest was identified in the Final Act of the Congress of Vienna of 9 June 1815, and consistently in later peace treaties, including the Treaty of Versailles (1919). The PCIJ defined community of interest in a navigable river as the

> basis of a common legal right, the essential features of which are the perfect equality of all riparian States in the use of the whole course of the river and the exclusion of any preferential privilege of any one riparian State in relation to the others.[78]

76 Sevette, *supra* note 1, at 321/322.
77 *River Oder Case, supra* note 59.
78 *Id.*

The PCIJ judgment in the *River Meuse Diversion Case* (1937)[79] related to a long-standing controversy between the Netherlands and Belgium regarding the diversion of Meuse waters to serve the Campine Canal, which had been settled by a treaty concluded on 12 May 1863. The treaty was concluded 'to settle permanently and definitely the regime governing diversions of water from Meuse for the feeding of navigation canals and irrigation channels' (preamble of the treaty). This case was related to the implementation of that treaty. The PCIJ ruled:

> As regards such canals, each of the two States is at liberty, in its own territory, to modify them, to enlarge them, to transform them, to fill them in and even to increase the volume of water in them from new sources, provided that the diversion of water at the treaty feeder and the volume of water to be discharged therefrom to maintain the normal level and flow in the Zuid-Willemsvaart is not affected.[80]

The PCIJ judgment in the *Case Concerning the Factory at Chorzów* (1928)[81] has sometimes been cited as the source of international law concerning award of compensation for injuries of a physical nature caused by pollution. Noting that the award may include consequential damage as well as direct loss, Antony Lester commented in the late 1960s:

> However, in many cases of international river pollution, [compensation for] damages alone will not be an adequate remedy, since the aim will be to prevent further pollution rather than to obtain monetary compensation. In such circumstances, the desirable remedy would be for an international tribunal to grant injunctive relief, restraining the defendant state from persisting in unlawful acts of pollution, and, if necessary, requiring the offending state to take affirmative action to prevent further pollution.[82]

---

79 *Diversion of Water from Meuse* (*Netherland v. Belgium*), PCIJ Ser. A/B No. 70 (1937). For details *see infra* note 110 and accompanying text.

80 *Id.*, para. [91].

81 PCIJ Ser. A No. 17, (Sept. 13), (1928), https://www.icj-cij.org/files/permanent-court-of-international-justice/serie_A/A_17/54_Usine_de_Chorzow_Fond_Arret.pdf.

82 A. Lester, *'Pollution'*, in A. H. Garretson, R. D. Hayton & C. J. Olmstead (eds.), *The Law of International Drainage Basins* (Dobbs Ferry, NY: Oceana Publications, 1967), 89–123, at 113.

The ICJ judgment in the *Corfu Channel Case* (1949)[83] has been relevant for identification of the rule of international law imposing general limitation of actions in the territory of one state that could cause injury in another state.[84]

Several arbitral awards complete this picture, the best known being the the *Trail Smelter Case*.[85] The case concerned transboundary sulphur dioxide air pollution from a Canadian zinc and lead smelter in the United States. The Tribunal found that

> under the principles of international law, as well as of the law of the United States, no State has the right to use or permit the use of its territory in such a manner as to cause injury by fumes in or to the territory of another or the properties or persons therein, when the case is of serious consequence and the injury is established by clear and convincing evidence.[86]

The *Lake Lanoux* arbitral award (1957),[87] resolving a long-standing controversy between Spain and France regarding diversion of the waters of Lake Lanoux, was delivered on 16 November 1957. The project called for diversion of a certain volume of water from Lake Lanoux, which lies entirely in the French territory and is entirely fed by the Carol River and other streams having their sources also in the French territory, for the purpose of electric power generation on the Ariège River. On exiting the power plant, the waters were to be returned completely to the River Carol before the Carol enters Spanish territory by means of a five kilometre long tunnel from the Ariège to the Carol upstream from the outlet from the Carol feeding the Puigcerda Canal in Spain. The case pertained to implementation/interpretation of the Treaty of Bayone of 26 May 1866[88]

83 ICJ Rep. 4 (1949).

84 For more details, *see infra* discussion regarding Article X of the Helsinki Rules.

85 *Trail Smelter Case* (*United States v. Canada*), Arbitral Award, 16 April 1938 and 11 March 1941, http://legal.un.org/riaa/cases/vol_III/1905-1982.pdf.

86 *Id.*, at 1965.

87 '*Lake Lanoux Arbitration* (*France v. Spain*), *Arbitral Tribunal, November 16, 1957*', in Sir H. Lauterpacht and E. Lauterpacht (eds.), *International Law Reports 1957* (London: Butterworths, 1961), 100–142, at 130. *See also Lake Lanoux Arbitration* (*France v. Spain*) (16 November 1957) 12 R.I.A.A. 281; 24 I.L.R. 101 [*Lake Lanoux Arbitration*].

88 The Treaty on boundaries between Spain and France from the valley of Andorra to the Mediterranean (with Additional Act), Bayone, 26 May 1866.

and the Additional Act of the same day.[89] The Tribunal, referring to the Geneva Convention (1923),[90] found that

> [t]he rule that States may utilize the hydraulic power of international watercourses only on condition of a *prior* agreement between interested States cannot be established as a custom, even less as a general principle of law.[91]

Thus, international water law evolved through the decisions of different international courts and tribunals on various topics related directly or indirectly to shared watercourses.

3.2 *Judicial Practice of States*

Perhaps the most interesting source of ideas having a formative effect on the legal formulation of applicable principles of international water law has been the judicial practice of confederal and federal states in resolving disputes between their confederal/federal units concerning the use of their shared waters.

The oldest relevant intra-state boundary judgment the *Zwillikon Dam Case* (1878) concerned diversion of the waters of the stream Jonabach, which divides the Swiss cantons of Aargau and Zürich. For the purpose of developing power for use in a factory, a dam was built in the village of Zwillikon (in the canton Zürich). The diversion of waters for this purpose had an impact on the amount of water available downstream to the mills owners in the canton Aargau. They were deprived of sufficient water during normal working hours. The permitting of construction of the dam was conditioned that the loss by third parties 'was prevented by compensating works or that the parties reached an agreement.' A certain amount of money was determined for adequate compensation. Argau brought the case before the Swiss Federal Supreme Court (*Bundesgericht*), claiming that its rights had been infringed. The Court took up the decision in 1878, finding that the rights of Aargau were

89 The frontier between France and Spain was fixed by three treaties signed at Bayone on 1 December 1856, 14 April 1862, and 26 May 1866. The three treaties were completed by an Additional Act of 26 May 1866, *id.* In this case, the treaty of 26 May 1866 and the Additional Act of the same day are relevant for the boundary waters.

90 The Tribunal (*Lake Lanoux Arbitration, supra* note 87, para. 13) quoted Article 1 of the Geneva Convention as follows: '[The present Convention] in no way alters the freedom of each State, within the framework of international law, to carry out on its territory all operations for the development of hydraulic power which it desires'.

91 *Id.*, para. 13 (emphasis in original).

not infringed by Zürich, because it had made equitable provisions for the protection of riparian owners in Aargau.[92] Commenting on this case, Smith maintained:

> From the international point of view the question is not one of property, but of jurisdiction. So long as the sovereign power of the state is exercised in a reasonable and beneficial manner, its exercise cannot be vetoed by the assertion of any absolute proprietary right. The ruling of the *Bundesgericht* essentially rests upon the principle of the "equitable apportionment of benefits", which was later adopted by the Supreme Court of the United States.[93]

Resolution of interstate conflicts regarding shared waters in the United States can be achieved through the conclusion of interstate compacts,[94] by the enactment of statutes by Congress,[95] and through litigation before the Supreme Court.[96] Conflicts between states arise due to inadequate water supply to support population growth (due to contamination of existing supplies or maintaining instream flow in order to protect the chemical, physical and biological integrity of water resources), overly abundant water (e.g., when flood control facilities for protection of a downstream state should be located in an upstream state), and water quality deterioration (due to discharge of pollutants

92 The sum of money deposited for that purpose was considered satisfactory to enable mills owners to construct their own dam and to provide the necessary water at all hours.

93 Smith, *supra* note 28, at 40. The case was quoted as reported in *Entscheidungen des Schweizarischen Bundesgerichts* (1878) Vol. IV, at 34.

94 The interstate compacts based on Article I, section 10, clause 3 of the US Constitution have been adopted since 1783. The interstate water resources compacts of the nineteenth century exclusively related to boundaries, navigation, and fisheries. Water compacts regulating water allocation, pollution control, miscellaneous issues (single purpose ones, generally pertaining to flood control) and multipurpose (regulatory and development) compacts entered the scene in the twentieth century. *See* J. C. Muys, *'Interstate Water Compacts: The Interstate Compact and Federal-Interstate Compact'*, Legal Study 14, *National Water Commission* (*Report NWC-L-71-011*), (Washington, DC, 1971), at 5–7.

95 During the 1950s there was only one such act, the Boulder Canyon Project Act (Public Law No. 70–642, 45, Statutes at large 1057 [1928], Codified at 43 U.S.C. § 617–§ 617t. [1928]). *See* G. W. Sherk, *Dividing the Waters: The Resolution of Interstate Water Conflicts in the United States* (Leiden: Brill/Nijhoff, 2000), at 437.

96 Several cases were resolved by decisions of the US Supreme Court, the subject matter of were interstate conflicts (subject to the application of the equitable apportionment doctrine, which forms the federal interstate common law), as well as the disputes concerning interstate water compacts (which in many cases are also subject to application of the equitable apportionment doctrine). *See* Sherk, *id.*, at 3.

in an upstream state).[97] The Supreme Court decisions in several cases will be discussed here.

The first decisions taken by the Supreme Court were in cases regarding use of the waters of the Arkansas River (1902 and 1907) by the states of Colorado and Arkansas. Colorado is an upper basin state that had adopted prior appropriation water rights doctrine. Kansas is a downstream state that had adopted riparian water rights doctrine. Recalling the riparian rights doctrine, Kansas required Colorado to provide full natural flow of the Arkansas River. To the contrary, Colorado contended that it was justified 'if her geographical situation and material welfare demand it to consume for beneficial purposes all waters within her boundaries', and that 'as the sources of the Arkansas River are in Colorado, she may absolutely and wholly deprive Kansas and her citizens of any use of a share in the waters of that river'.[98] Applying the '[f]ederal law, state law, and international law, as exigencies of the particular case may demand',[99] the Court chose to apply neither states' water rights doctrine, but established the doctrine of equitable apportionment of the benefits between two states resulting from the flow of water.[100]

The Court was consistent in using this approach in later cases. In a case involving Wyoming and Colorado (1922), with both applying prior appropriation of water rights for a project in Colorado to divert trans-basin waters of the Laramie River, the Court found that application of the cardinal rule, according to which priority of appropriation gives superiority of rights, should be examined. It decided the controversy needed to be resolved not 'other than eminently just and equitable to all concerned.'[101] A limited appropriation approach was applied, recognizing senior water rights in both states. On that basis, Colorado and Wyoming were both awarded a 'mass allocation' of water.[102]

The Court was consistent in a 1931 case involving two riparian water rights states, Connecticut and Massachusetts, regarding a plan by Massachusetts to divert the waters of the Connecticut River for the use in the Boston area.[103] This was the first case regarding equitable apportionment. The Court refused

---

97 Sherk, *id.*, at 1.

98 *Id.*, Appendix A-9, at 213, *Kansas v. Colorado*, No. 10, Original, 185 U.S. 125, 22 S.Ct. 552 (1902).

99 *Id.*, at 4.

100 *Id.*, Appendix A-9, at 244, *Kansas v. Colorado*, No. 3, Original, 206 U.S. 46, 27 S.Ct. 655 (1907).

101 *Id.*, Appendix A-22, at 415, *Wyoming v. Colorado*, No. 3, Original, 259 U.S. 419, 42 S.Ct. 552 (1922).

102 *Id.*, at 5.

103 *Id.*, Appendix A-7, at 195, *Connecticut v. Massachusetts*, No. 12, Original, 282 U.S. 660, 51 S.Ct. 286 (1931).

to apply the riparian water rights doctrine. The Court recalled the doctrine of equitable apportionment formulated in *Kansas v. Colorado* (1902, 1907) and *Wyoming v. Colorado* (1922):

> The determination of the relative rights of contending States in respect of the use of streams through them does not depend upon the same considerations and is not governed by the same rules of law that are applied in such States for the solution of similar questions of private right. [1902] [...] As was shown [in the 1907 case], such disputes are to be settled on the basis of equality of right. But this is not to say that there must be an equal division of the waters of an interstate stream among the States through which it flows. It means that the principles of right and equity shall be applied having regard to the 'equal level or plane on which all the States stand, in point of power and right, under our constitutional system,' and that, upon a consideration of the potential laws of the contending States and all other relevant facts, this Court will determine what is an equitable apportionment of the use of such waters [1922].[104]

The same approach can be identified in other litigation cases resolved by the US Supreme Court.[105]

In this context, the judgment of the Supreme Court of German Reich (*Staatsgerichtshof für das Deutsche Reich*) in the *Donauversinkung Case* (18 June 1927) is important. The controversy between two *Länder* concerned percolation of the Danube waters through the chalky river bed between the towns of Bräunlingen and Hüfingen in Baden and the town of Fridingen in Württemberg. The waters rise to the ground surface in Baden as the small river Aach, which is a tributary of Lake Constance, enriched with industrial valuable mineral solutions. Due to percolation, the river bed in Württemberg, for some ten kilometres, dried up completely for 309 (in 1921) to 29 (in 1922) days. Both *Länder* took active steps to alter natural conditions in their sole interests—Baden to increase percolation, Württemberg to diminish or prevent percolation. Both took action before the Supreme Court, seeking to prevent the activities of the other. Württemberg, supported in this case by Prussia, also requested that Baden undertake measures to prevent increased percolation due to natural reasons. Due to a lack of the legal principles that would govern interstate right

104 After Sherk, *id.*, at 6.

105 Other cases include *New Jersey v. New York*, No. 16, Original, 283 U.S. 336, 51 S.Ct. 478 (1931) and *Nebraska v. Wyoming*, No. 6, Original, 325 U.S. 589, 65 S.Ct. 1332 (1945). For more details regarding these and other later cases, *see* Sherk, *id.*

in waters in the German Constitution and Civil Code, the Court relied on the general principles of international law and declared:

> With regard to the use on its own territory of a waterway owned jointly with another State, every State is subject to limitations based on general principles of international law precluding it from infringing the rights of another member of the international community. No State has the right to cause substantial injury to the interests of another State by the use it makes of the waters of a natural waterway.[106]

Further, the Court cited an accompanying principle:

> [A]n attempt must be made to apportion or measure the respective interests in an equitable manner, balancing the advantages gained by one state against the injury, or possible injury, caused to another.[107]

Basically, the judgment provided for an obligation to retain the *status quo*. The Court pointed out that the settlement of this dispute must be the subject of an agreement between two *Länder*.[108] Commenting on a situation when

> a State Government fails to apply, or even prohibits the application of, measures deemed necessary in the light of the recognized principles concerning the exploitation and regulation of waterways, with the result that the population of another State thereby suffers injury while the population of the first State is favoured, [the Court found that] such conduct is incompatible with the essential principles governing the comity of nations[.],

Sevette commented that the judgment

> appears to extend the interpretation of the principle of limitations imposed by considerations of good neighbourly relations to include not only the obligation to abstain from certain acts but likewise the necessity for taking positive action.[109]

---

106 After Sevette, *supra* note 1, at 77.

107 Smith, *supra* note 28, at 56.

108 *Id.*, at 57.

109 Sevette, *supra* note 1, at 77–78, respectively.

Certain positions of governments were also of interest. For example, Smith referred to the first [known] formal statement of a general principle of law applicable to economic uses of international rivers. This statement was made in a letter from the Government of the Netherlands to its ministers in Paris and London (30 May 1862) regarding the controversy caused by diverting waters of the Meuse River by Belgium to the Campine Canal. The diversion of waters led to the damage in the territory of the Netherlands (in terms of diminishing navigability of the Meuse itself, increased velocity of the current in the Zuid-Willemsvaart, and flooding in Noord-Brabant due to the discharge of water used for irrigation). Recognizing that both the Netherlands and Belgium have the right to 'make the natural use of the stream', the Government of the Netherlands pointed out that

> at the same time, following general principles of law, each is bound to abstain from any action which might cause damage to the other. In other words, they cannot be allowed to make themselves masters of the water by diverting it to serve their own needs, whether for purposes of navigation or of irrigation.[110]

Sevette made reference to the diplomatic negotiations between Bavaria and Austria regarding diversion of the Tiroler Ache River by Austria. The two states agreed that, in the case of a contiguous waterway, neither state enjoys exclusive rights over the total volume of water. General principles of law allow them to claim only half of the volume of water. Further, they also agreed that for hydroelectric development, it was desirable to seek common agreement on 'what manner of developing of hydroelectric resources of the waterway' would provide 'the highest yield from both the technical and economic standpoints'. They also agreed that if the most rational solution was not identified in sharing the volume of water, but, for example, in 'a division based on the gradient of the river bed', the right of harnessing of the hydropower by one state would be conditioned by the other state with sustaining economic interests and possible rights of individuals concerned. If such interests and rights were safeguarded, the right of harnessing the volume of shared water cannot be refused. These principles were re-affirmed in negotiations and agreements after World War II between the United States and the British Military Government in Germany, on one side, and the Austrian government, on the other, for the joint

110 Smith, *supra* note 28, at 217 (footnote omitted).

development of the hydropower in bordering parts of the Inn, Saalbach and the Salzach Rivers.[111]

However, at the beginning of 1950s, there was no consensus among international lawyers on which of the advocated theories could prove that there are rules of customary international law applicable to the use of international rivers.[112] When scrutinizing the IIL Madrid Declaration (1911), Smith found some 20 years earlier (1931) that 'the subject is clearly one which is not ripe for codification at present day'.[113] Nothing changed in that regard until the early 1950s with the above-mentioned public announcement by the team of the UN Secretary-General Trygve Lie.

In the new era of international relations that emerged following World War II, which was founded on the United Nations Charter, the world had to deal with several serious international disputes concerning international rivers. The rights of upstream and downstream states to use waters of such rivers[114] were at stake. International disputes in the 1950s included those related to sharing the waters of the Helmand River (between Iran and Afghanistan),[115] the Indus River Basin (between India and Pakistan),[116] the Nile River Basin (between Egypt and England, i.e., Sudan),[117] the Jordan and Yarmouk Rivers (between Israel and

---

111 Sevette, *supra* note 1, at 49–50.

112 Such rules include territorial sovereignty, riparian rights, prior appropriation, and equitable apportionment. C. Bourne, *'The International Law Association's Contribution to International Water Law'*, in S. Bogdanović (ed.), *International Law of Water Resources: Contribution of the International Law Association (1954–2000)* (London/The Hague/Boston: Kluwer Law International, 2001), 2–57, at 4.

113 Smith, *supra* note 28, at 158.

114 That is, rivers that flow from one state to another (successive rivers) and/or form the border between states (contiguous rivers).

115 Relations between the two states were settled in two arbitral decisions (1871 and 1903), but distribution of waters evolved with later development of dams and reservoirs in Afghanistan. *See* Eagleton, *supra* note 29, at 326.

116 The Indus River Basin, on which irrigation systems had been built and used for a few hundred years, was divided by the state border between the new independent states of India and Pakistan, intersecting with those hydraulic structures and leaving sources of water under the control of India. For more details, *see* John G. Laylin, *'Principles of Law Governing the Uses of International Rivers—Contribution of the Indus Basin'* (25 April 1957), World Bank Archives Disclosure Authorized, Folder ID: 1787921, *supra* note 71; Professor Richard R. Baxter (Harvard Law School), *'The Nile Basin'*, in A. H. Garretson, R. D. Hayton & C. J. Olmstead (eds.), *The Law of International Drainage Basins* (Dobbs Ferry, NY: Oceana Publications, 1967), at 256–297. For a contemporary account of the case, *see* S. Salman & K. Uprety, *Conflict and Cooperation on South Asia's International Rivers: A Legal Perspective* (London/The Hague/New York: Kluwer Law International, 2002), at 37–61.

117 Egypt wanted to achieve an arrangement that would include most of the waters of the Nile River Basin. At that time, relations between the parties were based on the 1929 Nile

Jordan),[118] and the Columbia River (between Canada and the United States).[119] Despite the fact that interstate relations regarding the use and utilization of these waters were regulated in some cases by international treaties, disputes arose during their implementation.[120] These disputes clearly showed that the applicable rules of international law on the use of international freshwater resources were not sufficiently developed and principles of international law, which the rules were/would be based on, had not been defined clearly enough to bridge the different views of the states involved and to ensure lasting and satisfactory peaceful solutions.

In brief, this was the context of this field of international law when the ILA started its half century of work on the law on international waters, effectively responding to the situation through its Rivers Committee. Eagleton identified all relevant sources of international law in his 'Preliminary Study Outline',[121] which was submitted to the ILA biennial Edinburgh Conference (1954) together with a proposal that the ILA undertake appropriate research and study.[122] The Conference resolved that a committee be formed to study the issue of inland water rights, and Eagleton was invited to undertake the presidency of the Rivers Committee. With that resolution, the ILA initiated its substantive and influential role in the development of international water law.

Part 4: Step-by-Step towards the Helsinki Rules

The ILA started its study of the subject of 'inland water rights and obligations of the states' at the Edinburg Conference in 1954. The final result, in the form of the Helsinki Rules (1966) was achieved through the gradual, step-by-step,

agreement (which was based on the recommendations of the Nile Commission 1925). *See* Eagleton, *supra* note 29, at 327.

118 Syria and Lebanon were also involved, as were some other streams. *Id.*

119 The long legal history of relations regarding the Columbia and Kootenay Rivers between the two states, including details on application of the Harmon Doctrine in the Boundary Waters Treaty of 1909, is elaborated *in extenso* by C. Bourne, in the Part VI of his book *International Water Law*, *supra* note 28, particularly at 321–352.

120 Hayton had seen an explanation for such situations in the 'deliberate ambiguity' of certain treaty provisions, when the parties 'take a calculated risk in order to save agreement as whole', accepting 'provisions intentionally written in imprecise or vague language'. In that way, they postpone resolution of the problem until a more appropriate time by seeking clarification of ambiguities. *See* R. D. Hayton, *'The Formation of the Customary Rules of International Drainage Basin Law'*, in A. H. Garretson, R. D. Hayton & C. J. Olmstead (eds.), *The Law of International Drainage Basins* (Dobbs Ferry, NY: Oceana Publications, 1967), 834–895, at 835.

121 Eagleton, *supra* note 29.

122 *Id.*, at 331.

development of 'black letter' principles and rules drafted by the Rivers Committee. Throughout this process, the work of the Committee was carefully guided, supervised, and ultimately approved by several ILA conferences. This part documents the entire process of the Rivers Committee in fulfilling its mission.

4.1 *The Dubrovnik Statement of Principles*

4.1.1 Preparatory Work

The basis of the Rivers Committee work was a preliminary standpoint that there should be agreement between states concerning their shared rivers based on the recognition that each state has sovereignty over its own territory, including the rivers therein, and that the sovereignty of states is to be limited. The application of the maxim *sic utere tuo ut alienum non laedas*[123] has been considered as being uncertain in particular circumstances. However, the binding duty of notification of other states sharing a river before diverting its waters has been seen as grounded in treaties and doctrinaire discussions in cases where such diversion is claimed to seriously injure other states and thus lead to negotiations for a settlement of these claims.[124]

At that time, the only recognized principle of international law was the doctrine of due regard. When utilizing the waters of an international river, a state must take into consideration the interests of other states sharing that river and must obtain consent from potentially affected states. Such consent is also subject to the principle of due regard for the interests of other states and cannot be withheld contrary to such regard.[125]

The terms of reference of the Rivers Committee encompassed all inland waters. However, in its first report, the Committee limited its attention to international rivers, especially to newer uses such as hydropower generation, irrigation, and pollution. The Chairman of the Committee, Eagleton, wanted the Committee to recommend the legal principles on which rules of law could be formulated. However, not all Committee members supported this position.[126] Recently declassified and digitized documents of the World Bank relating to

---

123 *'So use your own as not to injury another's property'*, B. A. Garner, Ed. in Chief, *Black's Law Dictionary*, Seventh Edition (St. Paul, MN: West Group, 1999), at 1690. The principle has its roots in the common law and can be traced from the earliest times. The Latin maxim itself was created by Sir Edward Coke (1552–1634), who combined the Latin expressions *honeste vivere, alterum non laedere, suum cuique tribuere*, and the common law principle. For more details, *see* E. E. Smead, *'Sic Utere Tuo Ut Alienum Non Laedas: A Basis of the State Police Power'*, 21:2 Cornell Law Review (1936), 276–292.

124 Eagleton, *supra* note 29, at 331.

125 *Id.*

126 *See* ILA, *Report of the 47th Conference* (Dubrovnik, 1956), at 216 and 233.

the Indus Basin Dispute[127] show that after the Edinburg Conference (1954), members of the Rivers Committee extensively discussed various topics included in the draft Committee Report prepared by Eagleton. This discussion did not only include the exchange of letters, but also the publication of articles focussed on the issues on the agenda of the Committee, and the submission of extended and exhaustive comments on the principles set forth in Eagleton's draft First Report and the report of the American ILA branch.[128]

Different (sometimes completely opposite to each other) views regarding even fundamental issues were not resolved before the submission of the First Committee Report to the Dubrovnik Conference (1956), and the proposed resolution to the Conference was not adopted unanimously.[129] The differences among the Rivers Committee members included the view that, in absence of agreement between states, there are no rules of international law that apply to the use of the waters of international rivers (S. M. Sikri, India).

Professor Paul Gieseke (Germany) called on the ILA to be careful when stating the principles because 'a statement of supposed principles of law which are not in reality carried through, would have the same fate as those' formulated in the IIL Madrid Declaration.[130] Knauth 'disagree completely with the argument that there is no law concerning rivers'.[131] Opposing the opinion of Sikri that the water in an international river belongs to one state to the exclusion of others, Qadir suggested that 'the water does not belong exclusively to

127 World Bank Archives Disclosure Authorized, Folder ID: 1787921, *supra* note 71.

128 *Id. See*, for example, J. G. Laylin (Member of Covington & Burling, Washington, DC), *'Principles of Law Governing the Uses of International Rivers—Contribution of the Indus Basin'* (25 April 1957); J. G. Laylin, *'Comments Submitted to the Committee of American Branch of the ILA on "First Report of the Committee on the Uses of the Waters of International Rivers"'* (4 May 1956); Hon. Mansur Qadir (Barrister at Law in Supreme Court of Pakistan), *'The Uses of the Water of International Rivers'* (27 August 1956); S. M. Sikri (Advocate-General of the Punjab [East Punjab]), *'Comments on the 1st Report of the Committee'* (22 May 1956); American Branch of ILA, *'Observations on "Comments on the First Report of the Committee" by Mr. S. M. Sikri* [...]*'* (3 August 1956). Mention should also be made to a paper by F. J. Berber, *'Some Methodological Considerations Concerning the Study on the Uses of the Waters of International Rivers'* (15 September 1957).

129 Annex I to the Report (the proposal of the text of Resolution). It was adopted with five abstentions. Professor Jaroslav Žourek (Czechoslovakia) requested that his name be entered as an abstention. ILA, *Report of the 47th Conference* (Dubrovnik, 1956), at 241.

130 *Id.*, at 219. The Madrid Declaration was developed and adopted after only two sessions, without broader preparation, and its principles were not adopted unanimously. As a result, it was inapplicable in many cases. Some commentators thought the Declaration only dealt with half the problem, i.e., with the political aspect (sovereignty of states), while the 'physical moment' (geographic unity of the area of application) was ignored as was the case in 'almost all the legal treaties on this matter'. *See* discussion of Hartig, *id.*, at 230–231.

131 *Id.*, at 240.

any State, but that it is available to all of them for such beneficial uses as do not interfere with beneficial uses of it by others'.[132] A similar view was also favoured by A. C. W. Beerman (Netherlands).[133]

Noting that between 'is' and 'ought', there is a room for 'might be', Dr. A. G. Donaldson (Office of Parliamentary Draftsman, Northern Ireland) supported the Committee Report indicating that

> without making definite statements about the present state of law, and without straying into impractical idealism [...] the Committee's Report does provide a basis on which a set of definite and authoritative principles could be erected.[134]

The usefulness of the reference to the maxim *sic utere tuo* was supported by Laylin, but was opposed by Gieseke[135] and Ahmed Mitwally Atabani (Attorney-General, Sudan).[136]

Dr. M. Vivod (Yugoslavia) questioned the use of the expression 'preventable pollution' and proposed that it be made more specific by adding the word 'reasonable'. Pre-existing uses and inclusion of tributaries of an international river were also at stake. Dr. Jovan Paunovic (Yugoslavia) advocated in favour of multilateral treaties regulating uses of international rivers instead of a system of bilateral treaties when more than two states were involved.[137]

These intensive efforts to reach consensus on the text of the first Committee Report, i.e. formulation and legal status of the principles of international law, were reflected in discussions at the Rivers Committee sessions[138] and well-documented in the Conference Report.[139] Besides commending the Committee for its work and adopting the Statement of Principles, the final parts of the Dubrovnik Conference resolution contain the decision on the scope of the Committee's work and certain requirements directed to the Chairman of the Committee and the Committee itself (see below).

---

132 *Id.*, at 232.
133 *Id.*, at 222.
134 *Id.*, at 218.
135 Gieseke referred to the contemporary edition of *Black's Law Dictionary*, which said that the maxim was 'a mere verbiage'. *Id.*, at 220.
136 Atabani maintained that 'employment of the maxim [...] in the realm of international law is an unnecessary innovation [...]', which shall only add 'to the state of uncertainty already existing instead of clarifying it'. He proposed the use of the 'restricted sovereignty' doctrine. *Id.*, at 229.
137 *Id.*, at 223.
138 Held in Dubrovnik on 29 and 31 August 1956.
139 ILA, *Report of the 47th Conference* (Dubrovnik, 1956), at 216–248.

4.1.2 The Dubrovnik Conference

The Rivers Committee submitted its First Report to the 47th ILA Conference (Dubrovnik, 1956). The Report contained the 'Statement of Principles upon which to Study Further the Development of Rules of International Law with Respect to International Rivers'. Sometimes called the 'Dubrovnik Principles' or the 'Dubrovnik Rules', the Statement elaborated on the work of the Committee, contributions of certain ILA national branches, and comments from ILA members.[140] Expecting the approval of the ILA, the Committee sought to 'study [a] more precise statement of the rules of law, their implementation and the administrative machinery required', which might serve as the basis for 'preparation of a model bilateral treaty, regional arrangement, administrative and technical assistance by United Nations and other international organisations' or in dispute settlement.[141] It was not the intention of the Committee to deal with and state the current rules of international law.[142] The Conference accepted this approach and adopted the Statement of Principles in its 3rd Resolution and commended them to the Committee as a 'sound basis upon which to continue study of the rules of international law with respect to international rivers'.

Principle I of the Dubrovnik Rules states that a river flowing between the territories of two or more states is an international river and recognizes the right of a state to exercise rights over the waters in its territory, but in accordance with the principles stated in the Resolution (Principle II). A state has a duty (it 'must') to exercise sovereign control over the international rivers within its boundaries with due consideration of its effects upon other riparian states (Principle III). Connected to this duty is the recommendation ('should') set out in Principle V that states, in reaching agreements or in tribunals resolving disputes, should 'weight the benefit to one State against the injury done to another', taking into consideration factors relating to a particular use. Five factors were listed 'among [possible] others':

- The right of each state to a reasonable use of water;
- The extent of states' dependence on the waters of that river;
- Comparative social and economic gains to each state and to the entire river community;
- Pre-existent agreements;
- Pre-existent appropriation of waters.

140 *Id.*, at x–xii.

141 Annex I to the First Report of the Rivers Committee, *see id.*, at 244–248.

142 *Id.*, at 216.

According to Principle IV, a state is responsible under international law for preventing, by its reasonable diligence, public and private acts that change the water regime or injure another state. Under Principle VI, a state planning new works (construction, diversion of waters, etc., or change of an existing use of water that might affect utilization of water by another state) must first consult with the other state, and when no agreement is reached, they should resort to a technical commission and ultimately, as necessary, to arbitration. States are responsible for damage caused by preventable pollution in another state (Principle VII). Finally, Principle VIII requires riparian states to work together to fully utilize waters of an international river, with the aim of assuring the greatest benefits to all, both from the viewpoints of the river basin as an integrated whole and the widest variety of uses.

The Dubrovnik Conference asked the Rivers Committee to continue its work on an enlarged basis. It authorized the Committee to:

- Re-examine formulated principles;
- Widen the scope of its work so as to cover all inland waters of international concern, including artificial waterways, whether or not serving maritime navigation;
- Cover all uses, including navigation;
- Formulate rules of international law; and
- Report thereon to the next ILA Conference.[143]

The Conference called on the Chairman of the Committee to appoint new members in consultation with the Executive Council and ILA branches. A request went to the Committee to issue its reports to the branches, to invite and consider their comments and the comments of others, and to submit its report and circulate it to ILA, not later than three months before the next Conference, to be held in New York (1958), together with the comments of various national branches. The Conference suggested that financial assistance be sought to facilitate the work of the Committee.[144]

The abundance of documentation, as well as the clear and precise instructions of the ILA Dubrovnik Conference regarding the work of the Rivers Committee, show the great enthusiasm and professional proficiency of the Committee members. The documentation also highlights the productive methodological excellency of the ILA in its search for viable solutions for this complex issue.

143 ILA, *Report of the 47th Conference* (Dubrovnik, 1956), at xi.

144 *Id.*, at xi–xii.

4.2 *The New York Resolution*

4.2.1 Preparatory Work

Having clear terms of reference set out by the Dubrovnik Conference, the Rivers Committee continued its activities in an intensified manner under Eagleton's chairmanship until the end of January 1958, when he unexpectedly passed away. Knauth agreed to carry on with Eagleton's work and to prepare the report for the forthcoming New York Conference. The Dubrovnik Statement of Principles was a fruitful basis for continued research into a particularly complex field of international law and the formulation of legally non-binding provisions of international law, that might be used as a guidance to the court in cases concerning interstate water disputes.[145] The time schedule for delivery of expected outputs was extremely tight (only two years). However, the work of the Committee continued with an unprecedented pioneer spirit of enthusiasm.

The correspondence between Eagleton and other members of the Rivers Committee shows that following the Dubrovnik Conference resolution, an extensive list of the topics was identified. Grouped in 'headings', the list prepared by Eagleton included such topics as treaties and state practice, waterways that should be included, uses covered, restrictions (concerning diversions, construction, past uses, future uses, etc.), and administrative arrangements.[146]

Berber focussed his attention on methodological issues,[147] recalling the prerequisites for fruitful scholarly research that have been 'basis of scientific progress throughout the world since the times of Bacon', namely,

> the desire to seek, the patience to doubt, fondness to meditate, slowness to assert, readiness to reconsider, carefulness to dispose and set in order; and as being a man that neither affects what is new nor admires what is old, and that hates every kind of imposture.[148]

On several occasions, Berber pointed out how important it is to distinguish between the *lege lata* and *lege ferenda*, i.e., between what the law is and what the law ought to be. In the international law context, he recalled the warning

145 *See* Dr. K. Krishna Rao, *'Statement to the Indiagram'* (21 October 1958), World Bank Archives Disclosure Authorized, File ID: 1787921, *supra* note 71.

146 For further details, *see* Eagleton's letter (attachment) to the Rivers Committee members dated 23 September 1957, World Bank Archives Disclosure Authorized, File ID: 1787921, *supra* note 71.

147 *See* Berber, *supra* note 128. Hayton will also address the methodological issues in this field in 1967. *See infra*, note 151.

148 F. Bacon, *De Interpretatione Naturae Prooemium*, c. 1603.

of Professor Stone, that if this distinction is neglected, international lawyers will not be able to objectively arrive at 'what ought to be' by wandering 'in the clouds of self-induced exaltation'.[149]

Berber also focussed his attention on distinctions between municipal and international law, and his analysis led him to the conclusion that 'equitable apportionment', as interpreted in decisions of the US Supreme Court concerning interstate waters controversies, 'is not a principle of international law, but an equitable principle, the basis of a decision *ex aequo et bono*',[150] which in international law can be applied only under a special agreement. Thereafter followed his brief and clear consideration of the conditions under which international treaties create customary international law.[151]

Laylin submitted a paper to the Rivers Committee elaborating on Dubrovnik Principles IV–VII.[152] Commenting on the applicability of the Harmon Doctrine,[153] he concluded that

> the Harmon concept that the territorial sovereign has the legal right to deal with an international river as it chooses has long been dead. Recent attempts to revive its ghost have collapsed. The benefits of a water

---

149 Berber, *supra* note 128, at 5.

150 *Id.*, at 6.

151 *Id.*, at 6–11. It is not possible to present details of his exploration here. However, it should be noted that elaboration of the issue, specifically focussed on international drainage basin law, was necessary due to the international controversies regarding non-navigational uses of the waters of international drainage basins. That necessity was satisfied some 10 years later, to a great extent by the paradigmatic study of R. D. Hayton '*The Formation of the Customary Rules of International Drainage Basin Law*' (1967), *supra* note 120. In his 'memorandum', concentrating the scope of the study on international drainage basins, Hayton presented his findings on the nature of international community, state practice, practice of international agencies, opinions of commentators, treaties and proof of general international law, and relations between rules and principles.

152 Laylin's paper, '*Principles of Law Governing the Uses of International Rivers—Contribution of the Indus Basin*', *supra* note 116, was prepared for the Fifty-first Annual Meeting of the American Society for International Law held in Washington, DC, 25 April 1957.

153 The Harmon Doctrine, an opinion given 1895 by Judson Harmon, then United States Attorney General, regarding the use of waters of the Rio Grande River (concerning a dispute with Mexico), has been considered as a basis of the doctrine of absolute territorial sovereignty. For an exhaustive account on the Harmon Doctrine, *see* S. McCaffrey, '*The Harmon Doctrine One Hundred Years Later: Buried, Not Praised*', 36 Natural Resources Journal (1996), 549–590. For specific details regarding the Harmon Doctrine in the Boundary Waters Treaty (Canada–United States) (1906), *see* Bourne, *supra* note 28, particularly at 287–352.

> resource of international concern must, as a matter of law, be shared equitably by the territorial sovereigns.[154]

Dr. H. Fortuin (Netherlands) strongly supported the importance and validity of the maxim *sic utere tuo*, which should be accompanied by rules on condemnation of abuse of rights, cooperation between riparian states, international administration, and arbitration.[155] One observation by Shabtai Rosenne (Israel) is interesting. He noted that 'various papers, which have been circulated, are clearly reflecting various political interests of their authors'.[156]

The strong work of the ILA in this field allowed Eagleton to obtain financial support from the Ford Foundation[157] to enlarge the Committee and to call a Committee meeting in Geneva in October 1957.[158] At that meeting, the Committee decided not to deal with inter-ocean canals, but rather to emphasis the uses of waters other than for navigation and to deal with an international drainage basin as an integrated whole. In the Committee Report to the forthcoming Conference, an attempt was made to distinguish between the notions of 'a river system' and 'a river basin':

> The distinction [...] seems to be that a *system* is the tracing of the course of stream-flow, such as one ordinarily see on a flat map or chart, resembling the outline of a tree, with its roots, with stem and branches,

154 Laylin, *supra* note 116, at 15.

155 Eagleton, excerpts from letters, at 4, World Bank Archives Disclosure Authorized, Folder ID: 1787921.

156 Eagleton, excerpts from letters, at 3, World Bank Archives Disclosure Authorized, Folder ID: 1787921.

157 ILA, *Report of the 48th Conference* (New York, 1958), at 29. Financial support of the New York University International Rivers Research Project continued after the Eagleton's death under Knauth's successorship. Olmstead continued the work of the Project and, when he became Chairman of the Rivers Committee after Knauth's death in October 1960, together with Professor Albert H. Garretson (New York University School of Law), he redesigned the Project, which resulted in more substantial funding from the Ford Foundation. The Project results comprised comprehensive studies on equitable utilization of non-navigable waters of international drainage basins, pollution (primarily legal aspects), administration, five river basin studies (the Columbia, Nile, Plata, Indus, and Colorado river basins), and three appendices with the ILA Helsinki Rules (1966), IIL Salzburg Resolution (1961), and the above-mentioned paper by Hayton on formation of customary rules of international drainage basins. These results were made available to the public in the well-known book, *The Law of International Drainage Basins*, A. H. Garretson, R. D. Hayton & C. J. Olmstead (eds.) (Dobbs Ferry, NY: Oceana Publications, 1967).

158 Pierre Sevette (UNECE Committee on Electric Power), Herbert A. Smith (U. K.), Dr. Eero Manner (Finland) and Professor Juraj Andassy (Yugoslavia) (IIL) also attended the meeting in Geneva.

> spinning out to their sources or tips; whereas a *basin* is an expression of the "relief" aspects of map-making, and extends from one "divide" in elevation to another "divide", or from crest to crest of mountains, hills and more elevations. In many details, the concept of a basin is not geographically or politically apt. For example, the political boundary distinction between Belgium and the Netherlands, dealing with the deltas of the Maas (Meuse) and the Rijn (Rhine) is not aided by the concept of a basin, whereas it is clarified by the concept of a system.[159]

For the time being, the Committee put aside the issue of shared groundwater. The work at the meeting in Geneva and the results (consensus and differences regarding certain issues) are fully reflected in the 2nd Report of the Committee, which was completed by Knauth on the basis of Eagleton's work and discussed by the Committee at a meeting held in The Hague.[160]

At the same time, the IIL decided to begin work on the international law on waters. Professor J. Andrassy was appointed as the rapporteur of the IIL Ninth Commission on *Utilisation des eaux internationals non maritimes (en dehors de la navigation)*. He also produced materials for the ILA Rivers Committee[161] and, at The Hague Committee meeting, submitted 'excellent materials'[162] that were very welcomed by the Committee members.[163] A year earlier (1957), as a result of growing interest in the legal aspects of the use of international waters the Inter-American Bar Association had adopted a resolution on the principles of law that regulate the use of international rivers.[164] Also, the arbitral award in the *Lake Lanoux Case* was delivered in 1957.[165]

The results of the work of the Rivers Committee presented at the meeting in The Hague were discussed at meetings of the Committee held in New York just before the beginning and during the ILA Conference.[166] Different views

159 ILA, *Report of the 48th Conference* (New York, 1958), at 75.

160 28–30 May 1958.

161 ILA, *Report of the 48th Conference* (New York, 1958), at 29.

162 *Id.*

163 The work of the ILA and IIL concerning international waters was coordinated such that members of both organizations had full access to the research results. For a comprehensive insight into the work of IIL, including all of the reports by Andrassy, correspondence among the members, and discussions at their sessions, *see Annuaire de l'Institut de Droit International*, Volume 48 I (1959) and Volume 49 I and 49 II (1961). Reprinted by Schmidt Periodicals GmbH (Bad Feilnbach, Germany, 2001), http://www.idi-iil.org/en/publications-par-categorie/annuaires/.

164 *Supra* note 75.

165 *Supra* note 87 and accompanying text.

166 The New York Committee meetings were held 31 August and 1–3 September 1958.

among the members of the Committee persisted even at that stage of the work. The Committee Report submitted to the ILA Conference[167] show the span of differences, including the view of Professor Myres McDougal (United States) that the proposal to be submitted to the New York Conference was a 'retrogression' from the Dubrovnik Statement of Principles, and that it was not 'very positive' and could not be considered the final result of the ILA's work, but could be accepted as 'a basis for an advanced study of the matters concerned', as Manner maintained. Dr. Guillermo Cano (Argentina) expressed his disappointment with the Report of the Committee saying that

> [l]ittle or no contribution will be made to the progress of international law by writing cryptic sentences where most of the meanings lies between the lines. Worse still: what has been left unsaid is more important than what has been expressed.[168]

Sikri sustained his previously discussed opinion that the Harmon Doctrine is still the law. However, as a member of the ILA, he agreed to participate in making the relations of states more viable and supported the Report. Bourne noted the importance of the unanimous refusal of the Committee to recognize that a state 'may do as it pleases with the waters in its territory, and pay no heed to the consequences across its borders if what it does', and favoured acceptance of the reasonable and equitable utilization principle, proposing also that diversions from river systems be addressed.[169]

William L. Griffin (United States) was of the opinion that with the proposal for the New York Conference, a great step forward had been made due to the recognition that there are rules of customary international law that govern drainage basins. Those rules comprise the right of each riparian state to a reasonable and equitable share in beneficial uses, riparian states have duty to refrain from unilateral changes that may affect adversely the legal rights of others, and the right to resolve disputes by consultation or third-party processes. He also pointed out that there is no rule of law giving a veto on development projects.[170]

At this point, a specific issue deserves to be highlighted. The Committee already accepted, at its meeting in Geneva, the concept of the international drainage basin as the most suitable natural area for implementation of the

167 Dated 6 September 1958.
168 ILA, *Report of the 48th Conference* (New York, 1958), at 64.
169 *Id.*, at 37–38.
170 *Id.*, at 43–44.

rules on shared waters. However, the idea of inter-basin transfers of waters had been promoted by Bourne at the Committee session in New York:

> I shall comment on one point in the report. It is definition of "drainage basin". It is confined to natural drainage basins. I would suggest that, in view of present engineering skill which makes it possible to transfer the waters of one river basin to another, one has to consider the use of waters of an area rather than of a particular natural drainage basin. In determining what is an equitable share in the waters of a river, a most relevant factor is the issue that can be made of it by the riparian States, and so diversions to or from a river system ought to be embraced in this definition.[171]

The idea of broadening the definition of the basic territorial concept was not accepted by the Rivers Committee, and was never scrutinized by the ILA. This issue will be discussed further below in a context that emerged some 60 years later.

At the session of the Rivers Committee in New York, Professor Maxwell Cohen (Canada) pointed out the significance of exchange of information between riparian countries, while Judge Algot Bagge (Sweden) stressed the respective procedural arrangements. B. Cheng (United Kingdom) indicated presence of the general principle of law in terms of good faith, and Major Louis M. Bloomfield, Q.C. (Canada) highlighted the importance of regional agreements and treaty practice between riparian states. Dr. Dante A. Caponera (Italy) formulated the proposal for the Committee to shift its focus from the concept of 'international river' to 'international drainage basin' and called for the multidisciplinary collaboration of lawyers, engineers, economists, public health officials etc., on rivers and water resources issues.[172] Klaus W. Cuperus (Netherlands) proposed that further studies 'be undertaken to see whether differences between states should be solved in accordance with Article 33 of the UN Charter or whether it is possible and advisable to establish rules for a more practical arbitration machinery'.[173] Dr. Gerald FitzGerald (Canada) quoted Professor Jessup (United States), who commented that

> development must come about through the gradual emergence of improvements to existing legal principles, or to the cautious preparation of

171 *Id.*, at 57.

172 *Id.*, at 50–51.

173 *Id.*, 49.

> new legal principles where no rules on a particular subject have hitherto existed.

He also recalled the opinion of Professor Cohen who:

> indicated that the Association in attempting a statement of legal principles, must first carry out a scientific survey to ascertain the *lex lata*, and then try to fill in the gap between *lex lata* and what was considered to be desirable by a process of understanding and good will.[174]

He expressed the view that the Committee Report 'represents arduous effort on the part of the Committee and a sacrifice on the part of some of its members, of some cherished ideas'.[175]

The Committee invested great effort into overcoming differences of opinion with a view to unanimous acceptance of the text, the moral value of which Qadir highlighted. In searching for such consensus, Berber supported the integrity of the Report and Rao gave up his own proposals in favour of compromise and unanimity. ILA Secretary General W. Harvey Moore, Q.C. (United Kingdom), recalled the motto of ILA *Multis Melior Pax Una Triumphis*,[176] while the ILA President Oscar R. Houston (United States), expressed his view of the work of the Committee with these words:

> I have never seen a body of men who approached a difficult problem with fairer minds or with a greater willingness to subordinate personal views to the goal of achieving an acceptable solution than did this Committee.[177]

The Chairman and Rapporteur of the Committee, Knauth stressed that the Committee at the New York meeting 'has worked with remarkable devotion', and expressed his conviction that the

> [w]ater is essential to life, food, industry and transportation. We have here a universal physical subject of life and survival, a cause of deep-seated emotions and conflict to which the rule of law must be applied in the interest of peaceful relations and orderly purpose.[178]

174 *Id.*, 45–46.

175 *Id.*, 47.

176 *One peace is better than many triumphs.*

177 ILA, *Report of the 48th Conference* (New York, 1958), at 61.

178 *Id.*, at 30.

He submitted the unanimous proposal of the Rivers Committee, which he referred to as the 'New York Unanimous Minima', to the New York Conference.[179] The Conference adopted this break-through proposal as the Resolution on the Uses of the Waters of International Rivers (New York Resolution or Resolution 1)[180] with no dissenting votes. With this, the Rivers Committee accomplished the task assigned to it as 'described in the Dubrovnik 1956 resolution as a restudy of the Dubrovnik Principles'.[181] The New York Resolution also established the grounds for further work by the Committee.[182]

4.2.2 The Scope and Contents of the New York Resolution

Resolution 1 was composed from the text of three groups of legally non-binding norms: four heads of unanimous agreement, four statements on agreed principles of international law (*lex lata*) and 10 recommendations (which include *lex ferenda*).

The heads of unanimous agreement state that the immediate purpose of the ILA was to put forward some principles and some recommendations (first); there are customary rules of conventional and customary international law governing the waters of drainage basins that are in the territories of two or more states (second); and there may be issues not adequately covered by recognized rules of international law and that there are rules whose meaning is interpreted differently (third). Finally, the fourth agreed head offers a definition of the international drainage basin, which after some refinement to the text was adopted as Article II of the Helsinki Rules.

The statement on the agreed principles of international law comprises the *lex lata* principles. The first principle is that a system of rivers and lakes in a drainage basin should be treated as an integrated whole (not piecemeal). However, it should be noted that this relates only to inland surface waters. An agreed comment attached to the definition of this principle states that 'it may be necessary to consider the interdependence of all hydrographical and demographic features of the drainage basin'. Indeed, the ILA will consider this issue later.

The second principle is that each co-riparian state is entitled to a reasonable and equitable share in the beneficial uses of waters of an international

179 Third Committee Report, in ILA, *Report of the 48th Conference* (New York, 1958), at 99–101.

180 Resolution 1 was adopted on 7 September 1958. *Id.*, at viii–x.

181 Knauth's letter *'To the members of the 1957–1958 Rivers Committee'*, World Bank, File ID: 1787921, *supra* note 71.

182 Resolution 1, *supra* note 180.

drainage basin. This principle always applies subject to other provisions in a treaty or other instrument, or by customs binding the co-riparian states.

The third principle expresses the duty of all co-riparian states to respect the legal rights of each co-riparian state in the drainage basin. This encompasses the duty to prevent others for whose acts it is responsible under international law from violating the legal rights of the other co-riparian states (this is the fourth principle).

The 10 recommendations are composed so as 'to include' *lege ferenda.* No distinction was made between formulations expressing unanimous agreement on 'what the law ought to be' and the desirable behaviour or activity of certain subjects. There is no doubt that a *lege ferenda* rule is expressed by the Recommendation 1, which states that the co-riparian states should refrain from unilateral acts or omissions that affect adversely the legal rights of a co-riparian state in the drainage basin. This restraint is conditional on the willingness of the co-riparian state to participate in resolving differences as to their rights within a reasonable time. In case of failure to reach an agreement, involved parties should seek a solution in accordance with Article 33 of the UN Charter.[183] In a similar nature, Recommendation 3 requires the co-riparian states ('should') to make available to the 'appropriate agencies of UN' and to one another hydrological, meteorological, and economic information, particularly regarding streamflow, quantity and quality of water, rain and snow fall, water tables, and underground water movements. Further, Recommendation 8 requires the states ('should') to take immediate action to prevent further pollution and to study and put into effect all practical means of reducing present uses that led to pollution.

It is with less certainty that several other recommendations can be considered *lege ferenda.* Their structure and formulations indicate their desirable 'good practice' nature more than offering the possibility of becoming binding customary rules of international law. For example, Recommendation 2 expresses the hope that legal information concerning drainage basins will be assembled, exchanged, and disseminated by the UN and its specialized agencies that perform similar activities. Recommendation 4 would also fall into this group as it requires riparian states ('should') to establish by agreement

183 Article 33 of the UN Charter reads:

1. The parties to any dispute, the continuance of which is likely to endanger the maintenance of international peace and security, shall, first of all, seek a solution by negotiation, enquiry, mediation, conciliation, arbitration, judicial settlement, resort to regional agencies or arrangements, or other peaceful means of their own choice.
2. The Security Council shall, when it deems necessary, call upon the parties to settle their dispute by such means.

permanent or *ad hoc* agencies for the continuous study of all problems arising out of the use, administration, and control of the waters of drainage basins. Those agencies should be instructed to submit their reports to the competent authorities of the riparian states. In the same category, Recommendation 5 calls on drainage basin states to seek advice from technical experts when prioritizing uses of water. Recommendation 6, requiring competent authorities of co-riparian states to endeavour ('should') to resolve by agreement all matters which recommendations are made by technical experts, and Recommendation 7, requiring that every effort be made to reach agreement at a regional level, are obviously of the 'good practice' nature.

Recommendations 9 and 10 are quite different. Respectively they express the desirability for further study of the, *inter alia*, legal matters 'bearing on the prospective operation of the existing and desired rules of international law relating to the uses of waters of international drainage basins', and encourage the search for funding of research activities and consideration of how and to what extent further work can be carried out in harmony with similar work of the IIL and the Inter-American Bar Association.

It should be noted that, with the adoption of the New York Resolution, the legal differentiation between successive and contiguous international rivers lost its importance in international water law as concerns non-navigational issues.

From a contemporary perspective, the New York Resolution clearly can be seen as a reliable, firm, and promising cornerstone upon which the dedicated members of the ILA built further principles and rules of a new body of international law, which became known as the Helsinki Rules. However, the differences elaborated on concerning the legal nature of certain recommendations did not have any specific practical importance. All heads of the unanimous agreement, the statements of the agreed principles and recommendations served their primary purpose, namely, to be precious input into the further efforts of the ILA in this field.

4.3 *The Hamburg Resolution*

4.3.1 Preparatory Work

After the New York Conference, the work of the Rivers Committee continued with increased intensity. Small groups, called 'working parties', were formed for the study of specific issues, and their rapporteurs were appointed.[184] At the

184 With the aim to submit their reports to the Hamburg Conference (1960), the following reports were presented to the Committee (with feedback from ILA members and national branches): Rapporteur Cohen, Non-Navigable Uses, [and Donaldson, as the *ad hoc*

meetings in Hamburg[185] the Committee unanimously decided to maintain 'the unanimity achieved at New York' in its work and 'to "stick to" the New York 1958 text without any change'.[186] However, this was understood not to limit the Rivers Committee from further elaboration of procedural rules. At the same time, the Rivers Committee continued to follow the progress in relevant initiatives around the world. It noted the formation of the UN Water Development Centre and its first report,[187] the conclusion of the Nile Agreement between the U.A.R. and Sudan in 1959,[188] the treaties between Italy and Switzerland regarding Lake Lugano (17 September 1955) and the Reno di Lei (18 June 1949) and Spôl (27 May 1957), progress towards settling relations between Canada and the United States regarding the Columbia River Basin, resolution of a dispute between India and Pakistan regarding the Indus-Sutlej Basin, as well as the bibliography prepared by New York University, which documented over 2,000 entries on waters and rivers.[189]

During the meetings in Hamburg and work on drafting the Recommendations on Procedure Concerning Non-navigational Uses and Recommendations on Pollution Control, differences of opinion among participants appeared. For example, Andrassy was of the opinion that New York Principle 2 (reasonable and equitable share in beneficial uses) was not a principle of international law, or at least 'is not a principle that is unanimously adopted. It is not recognized as such in theory and has not been followed in state practice', he maintained.[190] However, the discussion on the New York Resolution was ruled

adjunct Rapporteur at the Conference]; Rapporteur Cuperus, Pollution; Rapporteur Fortuin, Navigation (two reports and written comments by Giesecke); Rapporteur Baxter, Inter-Oceanic Canals (two reports and comments by the Israeli and the Egyptian Society of International Law); and Rapporteur Manner, Timber Flotation.

185 The meetings were held on 5, 6, 8 and 12 August 1960.

186 For details *see* the Rivers Committee Second Report submitted by the Rapporteur Knauth. ILA, *Report of the 49th Conference* (Hamburg, 1960), at 33–37.

187 Water Resources Development Centre, 'First biennial report', Special Supplement to Official Records of Twenty-ninth session of ECOSOC, UN Doc. E/3319, 29 January 1960.

188 Agreement between the United Arab Republic and Republic of Sudan for the full Utilization of the Nile Waters, 9 November 1959.

189 For details, *see* Knauth's report to the Hamburg Conference, *supra* note 186.

190 *Cf.* in this context the preamble and relevant articles of the IIL Salzburg Resolution (1961):

Article II

> Every State has the right to make use of the waters flowing across or bordering its territory subject to the limitations imposed by international law and in particular those which result from the following legal dispositions. That right is limited by the right of use by the other States concerned with the same river or watershed.

out of order by the Chairman of the Committee.[191] Considering the text of rules 3 to 5, L. C. Green (United Kingdom) was of the opinion that the proposed draft 'goes backwards rather than forwards', and showed 'a tendency to retreat from the position on arbitral procedure that has been reached so far.'[192] One of the issues discussed in detail was the question of whether there is a need for the Hamburg Recommendations to correspond to the International Law Commission (ILC) Model Rules on Arbitral Procedure (1958),[193] which were seen as a 'more complete and more refined solution to the problem of securing arbitral settlement than do the present rules'.[194] Dr. Vratislav Pechota (Czechoslovakia) did not support draft concerning procedure because

> in solving disputes arising out of the non-navigational uses of so-called international rivers, [the draft] introduces an element of compulsory arbitration, a concept which does not represent a realistic approach to the solution of this highly important question.[195]

Rao objected to the text of recommendations regarding procedure on non-navigational uses in terms of their incompleteness and favoured reference to the ILC Model Rules, but recommended adoption of the Committee proposal because they 'amplify the procedures mentioned in the second sentence

---

Article III

> If the various States disagree upon the extent of their rights of use, the disagreement shall be settled on the basis of equity, taking into consideration the respective needs of the States, as well as any other circumstances relevant to any particular case.

Recitals 3 & 4 in Preamble:

> Considering that the obligation not to cause an unlawful prejudice to a third party is one of the basic principles governing general relations between neighbouring countries;
>
> Considering that this principle also applies to relations deriving from the various uses of waters;

Text in: *Annuaire de l'Institut de Droit International*, Vol. 49, II, at 381–384.

191 ILA, *Report of the 49th Conference* (Hamburg, 1960), at 38.

192 *Id.*, at 41.

193 The ILC completed the Model Rules during its tenth session (28 April–4 July 1958), Doc. A/3859, and UN General Assembly recommended them 'to the attention of Member States for their consideration and use [...] in drawing up treaties of arbitration or *compromis*'. UNGA, 'Question of Arbitral Procedure,' Ass. Res. 1262 (XIII) (14 November 1958).

194 Dr. D. W. Bowett (Quin's College, Cambridge, United Kingdom), supported by Dr. F. Münch (Germany). ILA, *Report of the 49th Conference* (Hamburg, 1960), at 38–39 and 45–46, respectively.

195 *Id.*, at 49.

of the [1st New York] Recommendation and of the unanimous New York Resolution'.[196] Dr. A. H. Tabibi (Afghanistan) was of the opinion that there was no need for new ILA procedures after the ILC Model Rules had been recommended by the UN General Assembly. States should resolve their controversies through voluntary agreements and, in particular, through neutral technical and scientific commissions. He supported the approach that the unanimity of the New York Principles should be retained.[197] Dr. J. L. MacCallum (Canada) also gave up his objections and supported the draft resolution 'recognizing the value of a unanimous recommendation by the Committee'.[198]

Bagge explained that ILC Model Rules were studied during preparation of the Committee draft and that there 'were special considerations making it desirable to have special rules' regarding water use.[199] Speaking on the legal nature of the Committee proposals, Olmstead explained that

> these articles are being put forward in a complete context of volition; they are termed recommendations in the title, the preamble uses the operative verb "recommends", in no place is the verb "must" employed. Hence, the wording of the entire document indicates its voluntary nature.[200]

He pointed out that the Committee rules on procedure differ from the ILC Model Rules. Besides arbitration, they also envisage other procedures (consultation and conciliation) and ensure preservation of procedural flexibility so that states will be encouraged to seek peaceful means for dispute settlement.[201] Actually, the Hamburg Recommendations on the Procedure Concerning Non-navigational Uses were formulated on the basis of a draft of the International Convention on Non-navigational Rivers prepared by Bagge.[202]

Expressing an opposite view, I. I. Chandrigar (Pakistan) pointed out that

> [t]he New York Conference did not accept the principle of territorial sovereignty, which would have led to absurd results, and accepted the

196 *Id.*, at 37.
197 *Id.*, at 39–40 and 47–48.
198 *Id.*, at 50.
199 *Id.*, at 39.
200 ILA, *Report of the 49th Conference* (Hamburg, 1960), at 38.
201 *Id.*, at 40 and 45 respectively.
202 Soon after the Hamburg Conference, the Committee had procedural issues on its agenda again, albeit from a different approach and with a different outcome, as will be discussed below.

> principle that each co-riparian State is entitled to a reasonable and equitable share in the beneficial uses of the waters of the drainage basin.[203]

The draft Hamburg Conference resolution with both Hamburg recommendations was adopted by the Committee unanimously.[204]

The Rivers Committee also discussed the issue of navigation. The freedom of navigation on international rivers as a general principle of law should be, according to Fortuin, granted to all flags. H. E. Scheffer (Netherlands) explained that, more or less, freedom of navigation had been derived from the principle of the freedom of the sea. He doubted that it would be opportune to study further the possibility of revision of the Barcelona Convention (1921) and suggested that further studies on inland navigation should consider regional aspects of the issue. He also proposed that the topic of inter-oceanic canals be removed from the agenda of the Committee. The reasons for this were the fact that there are only three such canals (Suez, Panama, and Kiel), with each operating under a different legal setting[205] and with a specific connection to maritime navigation and the law of the sea, while inland navigation is a matter of inland transport.[206] Dr. Ursula von Köppen (Germany) highlighted the importance of considering the political aspect of inland navigation, and pleaded for examination of some well-known questions, adding:

> [T]hese studies should be directed towards the future and should not aim at trying to reappraise the exact meaning of a judgement under discussion in the past or revive quarrels which jurisdiction and literature have so far been unable to solve.[207]

Pechota stressed the importance of the issue of the access of land-locked states to the sea.[208]

The Committee also proposed the core principles that the working parties would deal with on specific issues and the topics (e.g., pollution in respect of health, industry, agriculture, related activities, and the floating of timber) that would establish the scope of its programme of work. With a note of

---

203 *Id.*, at 48.

204 Rivers Committee, '*Report on the Uses of International Rivers*', (revised, and adopted at the meeting held on 12 August 1960), reprinted in ILA, *Report of the 49th Conference* (Hamburg, 1960), at 33–61.

205 Professor Hamed Sultan (Egypt), *id.*, at 58.

206 *Id.*, at 52–54.

207 *Id.*, at 55.

208 *Id.*, at 56–57.

anticipation, the Committee stated that its final product would be 'comprehensive statements of agreed principles, recommendations, and propositions relating to the various uses of international rivers'.[209]

4.3.2 The Hamburg Recommendations

The Hamburg Conference adopted Resolution II on the Uses of the Waters of International Rivers,[210] with Annexes I and II, which contained respectively the Hamburg Recommendations on Procedure Concerning Non-navigational Uses and the Hamburg Recommendation on Pollution Control.[211] The Conference instructed the Committee to continue to work 'on the lines indicated in its Report, but to suspend its work on Inter-oceanic Canals'.[212]

4.3.2.1 *Hamburg Recommendations on Procedure Concerning Non-navigational Uses*

The ILA Hamburg Recommendations on Procedure Concerning Non-navigational Uses (Annex I, to ILA Resolution II) were approved taking into consideration the importance of peaceful resolution of differences between co-riparian states regarding their rights in respect of the waters of a drainage basin. These recommendations were developed further to the second sentence of the first agreed recommendation of the 1958 New York Resolution. The recommended procedures were applicable in the absence of any other agreement.

The first recommendation relates to consultation, which co-riparian states should resort to in case of a difference as to their legal rights or other interests. According to the second recommendation, if such consultation does not produce an agreement, the co-riparian states should agree to form an *ad hoc* commission with the aim of finding a solution likely to be accepted by the states involved (conciliation). The third group of recommendations (Recommendation 3 (a)–(d)) contains the rules on forming such a conciliatory commission (appointing members, choosing the president, cases when the President of the International Court of Justice (ICJ) or UN Secretary-General might be requested to make appointments, place of meetings, etc.). The forth recommendation pertains to the case when the conciliatory commission is not formed in a reasonable time (several reasons were mentioned) and the options that the involved parties can resort to in such a situation (i.e., agree to submit

209 *Id.*, at 35.

210 Resolution II was adopted with 68 voting in favour and 3 against. *Id.*, at 51.

211 Resolution II, paras. 2 and 3 respectively, ILA, *Report of the 49th Conference* (Hamburg, 1960), at xvi–xviii.

212 *Id.*, para. 4.

the dispute to an arbitral tribunal, or to a permanent court of arbitration, or eventually, to the ICJ). The fifth recommendation deals with forming an arbitral tribunal. The rules of Recommendation 3 (d), which contains the method of determining the place of meetings and of settling the rules of procedure, shall apply also to an arbitral tribunal. No person who was a member of the commission may be a member of the arbitral tribunal. The sixth recommendation contains rules on the award of such tribunals (written form, decision, rationale, expenses, compensation to the arbitrators). The seventh recommendation indicates that recourse to arbitration implies that states should consider the arbitral award as final and submit its execution in good faith.

4.3.2.2 *Hamburg Recommendation on Pollution Control*

The Hamburg Recommendation on Pollution Control (Annex II, to the ILA Resolution II), further to New York Recommendation 8, consists of two paragraphs. The first paragraph recommends that co-riparian states set up by agreement pollution control commissions for each separate drainage basin. The second paragraph recommends that preliminary studies should be made by appropriate agencies dealing with the control and abatement of water pollution, with an aim of defining the scope and responsibilities of such pollution control commissions.

4.4 *The Brussels Conference*

4.4.1 Preparatory Work

At the meeting in New York,[213] following the Hamburg Conference, the Rivers Committee concluded 'that there was a reason to believe that [...] it might be possible to carry development of rules and principles [...] beyond the New York Resolution (1958)'. It was concluded that 'long-range studies would be undertaken' in respect to newly concluded treaties dealing with the Indus, Columbia, Nile, and Uruguay rivers. The plan was to submit a further report to the ILA 1964 Conference. The next meeting of the Committee was convened at The Hague in 1961, where the draft reports on three topics submitted by the rapporteurs[214] of the working parties were considered in great detail. The statements of rules of law were agreed on,[215] with respective comments on each article. All three revised reports of the working groups and all proposals

213 The first meeting convened under the co-chairmanship of Olmstead and Baxter was held in New York on 14 January 1961.

214 The Committee was asked to prepare reports 'with black-letter rules of law with the commentaries'.

215 At that meeting (1–6 September 1961), the following draft reports were prepared and considered:

of formulated rules with commentaries were included in the Committee Report to the Brussels Conference (1962). Also, two interim reports were considered at the meeting in The Hague[216] and were to be included in the Committee Report to the Brussels Conference (1962) and to the following conference after completion of requested adjustments.

The Brussels Conference considered the first draft of several core elements of the document that was later to be approved as the Helsinki Rules. Following the resolutions from New York (1958) and Hamburg (1960), Bagge proposed the 'draft lines' in the form of the articles grouped into four chapters on non-navigational uses of the waters, water pollution, navigational uses of the waters, and settlement of disputes. He suggested that those issues be left open for further study by the Committee, with a final comprehensive report to be submitted to the conference in 1964.

The Committee requested that the Brussels Conference adopt resolutions 'affirming the substance of the material contained' in its Report and authorize the Committee to continue its work for the 1964 Conference.[217] The Brussels Conference took note of the Committee Report, expressed its tentative approval of the substance of the Report, taking into consideration the comments and suggestions of the members at the Conference, and requested that the Committee continue its work with a view to submitting a final and comprehensive report to the 1964 Conference.[218]

4.4.2 Articles on Settlement of Disputes

Following the Hamburg Conference and adoption of the Hamburg Recommendations, more information on dispute settlement was made available to the Committee, causing it to reconsider the articles adopted in Hamburg, with a view of 'giving them a maximum of contemporary relevance'.[219] It should be noted that the Committee changed its earlier position that principles and

- Baxter – procedural rules for settlement of disputes (for the full text of the report, *see* ILA, *Report of the 50th Conference* (Brussels, 1962), at 429–443);
- Fortuin – navigation (for the full text of the report, *see id.*, at 443–469);
- Cuperus (& Olmstead at the meeting) – pollution (for full text of the report, *see id.*, at 470–477).

216 Manner prepared the interim report on the floating of timber; Laylin prepared the interim report on the rights and duties of parties to a water dispute pending to its resolution by peaceful means.

217 ILA, *Report of the 50th Conference* (Brussels, 1962), at 427–428.

218 At this Conference, out of the context of the agenda, Dr. Ivo Murko (Yugoslavia) raised the issue of the disagreement as to whether or not New York Principle 1 was a rule of international law at the Conference. *Id.*, at 425.

219 *Id.*, at 429.

rules of international law should be discerned from recommendations and in the articles developed and submitted in its report to the Brussels Conference:

> In order to maintain the continuity of the text, legal rules or principles have not been listed separately from the statements which make recommendations or are hortatory in nature.[220]

The earlier firm requirement to maintain clarity of existing principles or rules of international law (*lege lata*) and what is considered to be international law (*lege ferenda*) was pragmatically sacrificed here in favour of a technically consistent and tidy text of articles and the 'completeness of the system of settlement proposed here'.[221]

Perhaps this is the only example in the entire ILA work relating to the law on waters of international drainage basins when ILA accepted revisions of formally approved recommendations in an effort to maximize the contemporary relevance of its position.[222] In accepting revisions and drafting a new proposal for the Hamburg Recommendations on Procedure Concerning Non-navigational Uses, at that stage of development of the international law on shared waters, the ILA demonstrated it methodological flexibility. This flexibility can be seen in the full transparency of its work[223] and the clear vision of its prospective objectives, a worthy achievement for an international organization.

---

220 *Id.*

221 *Id.* It was further noted that 'several of the Articles neither recommend nor create obligations but simply reflect existing obligations under other instruments, such as the UN Charter and treaties providing for the peaceful settlement of international disputes'.

222 Certainly, one could recall here the case of the Berlin Rules, which were conceptualized as an attempted 'revision of the Helsinki Rules'. However, this comparison would not work here. The Berlin Rules were a completely new product of the ILA, aimed to 'set about to provide a clear, cogent and coherent statement of the customary international law, that applies to waters of international drainage basins, and to the extent that customary international law applies to waters entirely within a State, to all waters as well'. At the same time, the Berlin Rules were ambitiously aimed at undertaking 'progressive development of the law needed to cope with emerging problems of international and global water management of the twenty-first century'; *see* ILA, *Report of the 71st Conference* (Berlin, 2004), at 338. Such an ambition (never seen before during the long journey of ILA into the field of international water law) makes the story on Berlin Rules much more complex and incomparable to revision of the procedural rules set out by the Hamburg Recommendations discussed here.

223 'Transparency of work' is used here in the sense that the alternative text of articles on procedural issues with comments, dissenting from the agreed proposal of the Rivers Committee, prepared by Bagge, was fairly and seriously undertaken. Indeed, it was submitted to the 51st ILA Conference (Tokyo, 1964) and published in its entirety in the Conference Report (at 203–214). *Cf.* a complete lack of transparency in case of the dissenting opinion

4.4.3 Articles on Navigational Uses of International Rivers

The rapporteur of the navigation working party, Fortuin, prepared the first report on navigational uses of international rivers[224] in accordance with the ILA 1956 Dubrovnik Conference resolution,[225] which had authorized the Rivers Committee to expand the scope of its work to cover navigation. The rapporteur was invited to submit a report with the view to 'redraft and bring down to date [the] 1921 Barcelona Convention'.[226] During the discussion on the first report at the Committee meeting in Amsterdam,[227] it became clear that revision of the Barcelona Convention would give rise to confusion. Therefore, it was concluded that issues regarding the existence of general principles of navigation and commerce and various principles governing other rights and duties of co-riparian states should be set aside and discussed separately.[228]

The second report on navigational uses was circulated to participants of the ILA Hamburg Conference (1960) and discussed at a subsequent Committee meeting.[229] The result was the accepted draft of ten articles with commentaries that formed the basis of the third report, which was submitted to the ILA Brussels Conference (1962). Having thoroughly reviewed historic and international perspectives on the freedom of navigation[230] on navigable rivers separating or traversing territories of two or more states,[231] the Committee concluded that

> the rule that each riparian State [...] shall have to accord free exercise of navigation to vessels flying the flag of any nation, has not yet been generally accepted as a principle of law.[232]

The Committee clarified several aspects of navigational uses connected to other rules of international law, particularly those governing non-navigational

---

of four members of Water Resources Committee to the Report, which contained the proposal for approval of the Berlin Rules. *See* ILA, *Report of the 71st Conference* (Berlin, 2004).

224 The report was dated 31 August 1959.

225 ILA, *Report of the 47th Conference* (Dubrovnik, 1954), at x–xii.

226 ILA, *Report of the 50th Conference* (Brussels, 1962), at 443.

227 28–31 December 1959.

228 ILA, *Report of the 50th Conference* (Brussels, 1962), at 443–444.

229 The Committee met in The Hague 1–6 September 1961.

230 The investigation comprised such issues as obstruction of innocent passage which hampers inland navigation on an international river, freedom of navigation only for the flags of the riparian states, and freedom of navigation to all flags (i.e., non-discrimination between riparian and non-riparian states).

231 For details see the ILA, *Report of the 50th Conference* (Brussels, 1962), at 443–452.

232 *Id.*, at 451.

uses. Thus, the articles on navigation not only have to be considered in conjunction with general rules of international law, but also in conjunction with the general rules expressed in the articles on non-navigational uses. In particular, the Committee stated that there is no principle establishing an absolute priority of navigation over other uses. Navigation is to be considered as one of the uses to which 'each co-riparian State is entitled to a reasonable and equitable share in the beneficial uses of the waters of the drainage basin. To these uses may also belong the free navigation'.[233] Further, three definitions specific to navigation were established, which differ from those pertaining to other uses (as discussed elsewhere in this study). The Articles concerning navigation are applicable to the clearly defined parts of international watercourses, except as otherwise provided by a treaty or other binding instrument or custom.[234] The dispute settlement articles were considered as providing guidance in navigational use disputes.

The freedom of navigation definition used here assumed that each riparian state was entitled to enjoy rights of free navigation on the entire course of a river or lake, subject to any limitations or qualifications identified in other adopted ILA rules.[235] The scope of the term 'free navigation' includes:

- Freedom of movement of all vessels of a riparian state on the basis of equality, on the entire navigable course;
- Freedom to enter ports and to make use of plants and docks; and
- Freedom to transport goods and passengers (directly or through transshipment) between the territories of two riparian states and between the territory of one riparian state and the open sea.[236]

These freedoms are subject to the rights of police of the riparian state (over the part of the river or lake under its jurisdiction), which include, and is not limited to, protection of public safety and health. Such rights of police do

233 *Id.*, at 451–452.

234 Article I (1) refers to those portions of the river systems that are navigable and separate or traverse the territories of two or more states (corresponds to Helsinki Rules Article XII (1)). Article II (2) defines a navigable river as a river that is currently used for ordinary commercial navigation in its natural or canalized state or is capable of being used for such navigation due to its natural conditions (corresponds to Helsinki Rules Article XII (2)). The term 'riparian State', as provided for by Article I (3), refers to a state through or along which the navigable portion of a river (and lake) flows (corresponds to Helsinki Rules Article XII (3)). *Id.*, at 453. Proposed draft Article II provides this exception.

235 *Id.*, art. (corresponds to Helsinki Rules, art. XIII).

236 *Id.*, art. III (corresponds to Helsinki Rules, art. XIII).

not include unreasonable interference with the rights of free navigation of other riparian states.[237]

In an attempt to clarify confusion resulting from the use of the terms 'grand cabotage' and 'petite cabotage', the respective provision was formulated as the right of a riparian state ('each riparian State may') to restrict or prohibit the loading by vessels of a foreign state of goods and passengers in its territory for discharge 'in such territory'.[238] A riparian state may grant rights of navigation to non-riparian states in the portions of rivers and lakes that are within its territory.[239]

A recommendation that riparian states take measures on a cooperative basis to meet the expanding needs of navigation[240] was not elaborated on further by the Committee and was not included in the Helsinki Rules. Vessels of war, those performing police or administrative functions, and, in general, vessels exercising any other form of public authority were excluded from application of the ILA rules on navigation.[241] Finally, in the times of war, other armed conflict or public emergency situation constituting a threat to the life of a state, a riparian state has the right (a 'State may') to take measures derogating from its obligations in accordance with other rules on navigation. The extent of derogation was formulated as 'strictly required by the exigencies of situation'. However, such measures may not be inconsistent with other obligations under international law. Humanitarian purposes must in any case be facilitated by a riparian state.[242]

Each riparian state 'is required' to maintain in good order the navigable portion of a river or lake within its jurisdiction. This requirement includes removal of any obstruction to navigation, dredging, and other hydraulic works necessary for preserving navigation, but also the right to use port facilities in a co-riparian state. However, there is no rule in international law that would bind the riparian countries to maintain and improve navigable waterways. Therefore, this requirement is not an unconditional duty, but is subject 'to the extent of the means available or made available' to the riparian state.[243]

---

237 *Id.*, art. IV (corresponds to Helsinki Rules, art. XV), which additionally included the aspect of protection of public safety and health.

238 *Id.*, art. V (corresponds to Helsinki Rules, art. XVI).

239 *Id.*, art. VI and Helsinki Rules, art. XVII.

240 *Id.*, art. VIII.

241 *Id.*, art. IX and Helsinki Rules, art. XIX.

242 *Id.*, art. X, second sentence (first sentence was omitted in further work) and Helsinki Rules, art. XX.

243 *Id.*, art. VII and Helsinki Rules, art. XVIII. For more details *see* the comment to Helsinki Rules Article XVIII and the comment to Helsinki Rules Article IV relating to beneficial use.

With regards to maintenance, the Helsinki Rules properly reflect the principle of freedom of navigation, which can be implemented in practice only by the collective action of all riparian states, as noted in previously completed detailed studies.[244] However, application of the second principle of international law relevant to improvement of natural waterways, namely, the requirement to resolve all issues affecting navigation by agreement, was omitted from the approved articles.

4.4.4 Pollution of the Waters of a Drainage Basin

The Rivers Committee has always considered pollution of waters of an international drainage basin in its deliberations. Cuperus, who was appointed rapporteur for this topic, submitted two reports[245] in accordance with the New York Agreed Recommendations 8 and 9. Recommendations in the second report were considered by the Committee[246] and three articles were formulated, with a view to addressing various kinds of pollution in international drainage basins.[247] The Committee sought to define water pollution of an international drainage basin,[248] set out the duty of a state to prevent or abate pollution, and determine the consequences for violation of such duty.[249] Cuperus prepared comments to the articles, supporting the proposals by referring to judicial and arbitral practice, treaty law, and theoretical views. The articles with comments were included in Chapter III (Pollution) of the Helsinki Rules as Articles IX, X, and XI.

A clear distinction between a 'statement of law (*lex lata*) and consideration of what the law ought to be (*lex ferenda*)' was made in the discussions on freedom of navigation at the Brussels Conference (1962). Opinions were divided about formulation of the scope of the right to freedom of navigation. At issue was whether the right should be granted to 'all vessels flying flags of a riparian state' (which was considered an established principle of international law) or to the 'vessels flying all flags' (a long-standing practice established by

244 *See* Fortuin's *'Report on Chapter Concerning Navigational Uses of International Rivers'*, in ILA, *Report of the 50th Conference* (Brussels, 1962), 443–469.

245 The first report was presented in October 1959 (as part of the Hamburg Conference Committee Report) and the second at the Hamburg Conference (which resulted in approval of Hamburg Recommendation II).

246 The second report was presented at its meeting in The Hague, 1–5 September 1961.

247 These sources included pollution from municipal sewage, industrial waste, and timber floating, as well as new sources of pollution (chemical, household detergents, agricultural sources, radioactive waste).

248 Draft Article I defined pollution as referring to any artificial and detrimental change in the natural composition, content, or quality of waters.

249 These duties were set out in draft Articles II and III.

conventional law and one that would be desirable as a principle of international law, i.e., *lex ferenda*). Dr. C. W. Van Santen (Netherlands) expressed the opinion that Rapporteur Fortuin's statement allowing free navigation on international rivers for any riparian flag and 'denying the existence of a rule giving the some right to any flag' is

> [r]egrettable and tending to frustrate a possible evolution of the more liberal rule which would be so much more in accordance with our ideas of the greatest possible freedom of movements among Nations.[250]

Scheffer was of the opinion that 'codification of the law is not a thing that should be done *in abstracto*', and, recalling Article 13 of the UN Charter, he maintained that 'codification and progressive development of the law can hardly be separated'. Therefore, on the basis of development of conventional law, 'which was regarded by many as an increasing recognition of a general principle of International Law, and which in practice is applied on numerous rivers and waterways,' he expected the right of freedom of navigation to be recognized in articles on navigation for vessels flying all flags, not just the flags of riparian states.[251]

Noting that the process of development of international law that 'would make the navigational uses of rivers open to all flags still is not a law', Dr. Nagendra Singh (Secretary to the President of India) asked for a reopening of the discussion:

> [I]f, in the enthusiasm to develop International Law, *lex lata* and *lex ferenda* are both mixed up, I would submit that it would spell complete confusion and disaster. [...]
>
> Resolutions attempting to develop International Law by confusing *lex lata* with *lex ferenda* will only go to shake the confidence of the developing countries by causing confusion, since such [a] statement of the International Law Association would not be supported by the recognized text books of International Law. [...]
>
> In future, therefore, it is the imperative duty of all jurists to maintain distinction between *lex lata* and *lex ferenda*. If law has to be developed, let us bring it under the category of recommendations *de lege ferenda*.[252]

---

250 ILA, *50th Conference* (Brussels, 1962), at 403.
251 *Id.*, at 403–404.
252 *Id.*, at 409.

Finally, on this issue, the ILA expressed only, in the opinion of the members present at the Conference, what was considered to be *lex lata* on navigation. In coming decades such a choice will be justifiable, considering that freedom of navigation for vessels 'flying all flags', more than a half century later, is still *lex ferenda.*

4.5 *The Tokyo Conference*

Following the Brussels Conference (1962), the Rivers Committee held meetings at The Hague[253] and London.[254] At the meeting in The Hague, the Committee considered the redrafted texts of the chapters on settlement of disputes (Rapporteur A. H. Baxter), navigational uses (Rapporteur Fortuin) and pollution (Rapporteur Olmstead). The new chapter with commentaries on timber floating, prepared by Rapporteur Manner, and the revised text of the statements of principles in these areas of study were also considered. The proposed text of the Committee report to the Tokyo Conference (1964) was distributed among Committee members and, after having received their feedback, a new draft was prepared on the basis of the discussion at the London meeting, particularly with regards to pollution.[255]

The issue of *lege lata* and *lege ferenda* appeared in discussions on the procedures for the prevention and settlement of disputes at a Committee meeting in Tokyo.[256] At that meeting, Bagge submitted a separate report that contained a set of 32 rules with comments on the chapters.[257] Dr. A. Weiss-Tessbach (Austria) noted that the two reports fundamentally differ from each other. The Committee Report 'seems to be a statement of existing international law, while Bagge's rules are a recommendation to the governments'.[258] As a pragmatic solution, he suggested that the ILA should 'refrain from making pronouncement as to the existing international law', because

> [i]t is somewhat easier for a State to comply with a recommendation than to acknowledge an individual solution as being based on international law. In acknowledging a rule to be a rule of law the States admit that the rule is applicable in any case and that the sovereignty of the States is thereby infringed.[259]

253 1–7 August 1963.
254 2–5 April 1964.
255 ILA, *Report of the 51st Conference* (Tokyo, 1964), at 165.
256 The meeting was held on 21 August 1964.
257 ILA, *Report of the 51st Conference* (Tokyo, 1964), at 203–214.
258 *Id.*, at 152.
259 *Id.*, at 152–153.

Replying to that approach, Baxter explained that drafting a set of rules which 'States might wish to adopt in order to regulate their relationships, does not reflect the assumption on which [the] Committee has proceeded during the eight years of its existence'.[260] Olmstead added, 'the books are full of suggested Conventions, and many still remain mere suggestions'. The Committee 'endeavours to restate and define general principles of international law that are applicable to this subject'.[261]

The chapter on pollution was the most difficult to finalize due to the fact that pollution was 'a major problem'.[262] The Committee tentatively adopted the chapter on pollution with a view to it being considered in relation to the definition of the concept of 'equitable utilization' or 'equitable apportionment' adopted by the Committee. In spite of plans to submit a final report to the Tokyo Conference (1964), the Committee needed more time to research and draft a chapter on equitable utilisation or equitable apportionment and to clarify some other issues. Therefore, the Committee indicated its intention to submit its final report to the 1966 Conference.[263]

Olmstead's report further scrutinized the three articles on pollution with attached comments.[264] After having defined 'pollution',[265] the duties of the state where the water pollution originated or, if the pollution originated outside of its territory but was caused by its conduct, were streamlined with the principle of equitable utilization of waters of an international drainage basin. These provisions comprise:

- The duty ('a State must') to prevent any new form of water pollution, or any increase in degree of existing pollution, that would cause substantial injury in the territory of a co-riparian state;

---

260 *Id.*, at 154.

261 *Id.*, at 156.

262 'The conflict of interest is most direct and the application of the rule of law would of course, not be completely pleasing to any interested state'. *See* Olmstead, *'Introduction'*, in ILA, *Report of the 51st Conference* (Tokyo, 1964), at 165.

263 The report was expected to include chapters on navigation, timber floating, pollution, dispute settlement, and 'equitable utilization' or 'equitable apportionment'.

264 The text of those provisions (Articles I–III) was only slightly changed to become with Articles IX–XI of the Helsinki Rules.

265 Article I of the chapter on pollution defines pollution as any detrimental change in natural composition, content or quality of waters of an international drainage basin, which is a result of human conduct. The same text is incorporated in Article IX of the Helsinki Rules. It should be noted that changes resulting from natural causes are excluded here, because the 'international law takes no cognizance' of them. *See* Comment to Article IX of the Helsinki Rules.

- The recommendation ('a State should') take all reasonable measures to abate existing water pollution to the extent that no substantial damage is caused in the territory of a co-riparian state;
- As a consequence of violation of those rules, the state responsible for pollution shall be subject to the requirements to:
  - cease wrongful conduct;
  - compensate the injured co-riparian state for the caused injury; and
  - promptly to enter into negotiations with the injured state (if it fails to take reasonable measures), with a view to reaching an equitable settlement.[266]

After a lengthy discussion about the draft resolution at the Conference, the text of the resolution was agreed to and the Conference 'accepted provisionally' the text and commentary of the chapters contained in the Committee Report. The texts of the articles in chapters on navigation, timber floating, pollution, and settlement of disputes were accepted subject to any changes that may be necessitated by the chapter on the equitable sharing of uses. The Committee was asked to continue its studies in the light of discussions at the Conference, particularly on the subject of equitable sharing of uses. The Committee also was asked to submit a final report at the next ILA Conference (Helsinki, 1966).[267]

Part 5: The Helsinki Conference

5.1 *Final Report of the Rivers Committee*

The Rivers Committee scrutinized its final report to the Helsinki Conference at three meetings[268] following the Tokyo Conference (1964). The Report was drafted within the scope of the New York Resolution (1958) in the form of 'a statement of existing rules of international law, coupled with certain recommendations concerning the conduct of nations within an international drainage basin'.[269] The Report contains a summary (explanatory) introduction pointing out the significance of the New York Resolution (1958). Some elements of the Resolution were seen as 'more important aspects', recognizing that

266 For details, *see* the comments to the respective articles in the Olmstead report on pollution, in ILA, *Report of the 51st Conference* (Tokyo, 1964), at 175–186, and Comments to Articles IX–XI of the Helsinki Rules.

267 *Id.*, at 162.

268 One meeting was held at Harvard (1965) and two in Helsinki (on 16 and 19 August 1966) before the ILA 52nd Conference session, which was held in Helsinki on 20 August 1966. The 52nd Conference adopted the Report with the articles and comments known as Helsinki Rules on the Uses of the Waters of International Rivers.

269 ILA, *Report of the 52nd Conference* (Helsinki, 1966), at 482–483.

> existing rules of international law do govern the uses of waters of international drainage basins and that problems relating to uses should be approached on the basis of the basin, considered as an integrated unit.[270]

Thereafter, followed the text of the proposed Rules on the Uses of the Waters of International Rivers.

During the meetings dealing with preparation of the Rivers Committee Report for the Helsinki Conference, certain important issues were clarified and numerous topics were identified for further study and codification. Referring to Article I of the proposed Rules, Laylin pointed out that all other articles 'are to be taken as stating customary law in the absence of a treaty or binding custom to the contrary'. Speaking about the relationship between existing and planned (new) uses, he recalled the 1958 Committee Report in which Eagleton informed the Committee that the American ILA Branch Committee had not found a single case where states declined to respect the right to the continued enjoyment of a lawfully established beneficial use.[271]

Justice M. R. Khan (Pakistan) maintained that the proposed articles did not sufficiently state the law on the uses of waters of an international drainage basin due to superfluity, omissions, and ambiguity. He considered that some comments deserved to be incorporated into the text of the articles, while others might be the basis for further considerations of a reconstituted Committee. This view was rejected by Olmstead who recalled 'the very strong and effective participation of H. E. Syed Sharifuddin Pirzada (Pakistan) in supporting formulated rules'.[272]

Rao noted that the article on the relevant factors for determining an equitable use recognized that there may be other factors in a particular case, and that all the factors should be considered together. He pointed out 'that rivers have their own individuality and require individual treatment'. In that context he maintained that 'there is no obligation on a State to deny itself any present reasonable use of the waters of an international drainage basin in order to reserve for a co-basin State a future use of such waters'.[273]

MacCallum set out for the Committee reasons why certain waters in areas that do not contribute to an international drainage basin, i.e., isolated water bodies whose waters are shared, should be excluded from apportionment between drainage basin states. Speaking in favour of a broader approach, he

270 *Id.*, at 481–482.
271 *Id.*, at 454.
272 *Id.*, at 463.
273 *Id.*, at 459.

highlighted the benefits of diversion of waters from a wholly national basin into an international drainage basin.[274] Dr. H. Zurbrügg (Switzerland) was of the opinion that it would be wrong to conclude that, in the context of reasonable and equitable share of benefits of a river basin, any diversion of waters out of a drainage basin would be considered illegal conduct by a state.[275]

Bloomfield expressed the opinion that history alone will judge whether the Committee's 'move on the new ground' was successful or not in making a contribution to the settlement of international rivers disputes.[276] Berber observed that

> it was refreshing to hear that each river has its proper individuality, that it is not international law which has created Nations, but that Nations created international law, that State practice is the main source of international law, that a regulation based on community of exploitation is the exception, not the rule in State practice, that we find international water law mainly in bilateral treaties, not in the opinions of writers.[277]

Berber emphasized that the articles reflect a diversity of opinions. They were not intended to bind a judge, but to be directives, 'which could guide and inspire negotiators of future water treaties'. He concluded:

> [A]s a compromise the Articles represent a delicate balance between widely divergent views. Any perfectionist attempt to change the hard-attained result of so many years of arduous labour would tend to undermine the compromise, would reopen all problems, [and] would destroy [the] delicate balance between widely divergent views.[278]

Weiss-Tessbach transmitted the message from the Austrian Branch of ILA that it could not support the Committee Report, because, in its opinion, 'circumstances in every drainage basin are so different that [...] no international laws have developed, which could be applicable in all circumstances' and because the definition of equitable utilization, as drafted by the Committee is 'so vague that it cannot be called a rule of law'. He proposed changing the text to recommendations.[279] In this way, the always present *lege lata* and *lege ferenda*

274 *Id.*, at 460–461.
275 *Id.*, at 461.
276 *Id.*
277 *Id.*
278 *Id.*, at 462.
279 *Id.*

issue, even at this stage of the work of the Rivers Committee, missed the opportunity to reduce confusion. This attitude was rejected by Olmstead, who reminded Conference delegates that the task of the Committee was to restate the rules of international law applicable to the use of waters of an international drainage basin.[280] This 'ghost' issue, which would persevere in discussions concerning international law on shared water resources long into the future, warranted continued attention within the Rivers Committee in the opinion of, for example, Professor Lars Hjerner (Sweden). He commented that 'the Report goes too far if it purports to present a restatement of what international law on this field actually is'.[281] Reacting to this approach, Cuperus stated:

> [I] care but little whether all or part of our black letter rules are rules of international law or whether they constitute an exercise in *de lege ferenda* draftsmanship. [...] [T]he main question is whether the ideas we have given juridical form to [...] can serve any useful purpose. [...] and it is my firm conviction that the outcome of our labour can guide, in a most useful and practical way, those who are entrusted with the task of finding appropriate and equitable solutions.[282]

Speaking on the principle of equitable utilization, Olmstead explained that the factors to be considered 'stand on equal footing'. They were 'listed only as an illustration and cannot be ranged in a hierarchical order'. He also pointed out that 'the natural community of interests among co-basin States is adequately protected in the equitable utilization approach to uses of an international drainage basin'.[283] Further clarifications were offered by Baxter, who emphasized that prepared articles 'are operative only in the absence of agreement. Throughout the Articles we emphasize the desirability of agreement'.[284] The articles would be a framework for agreements and would help in negotiations. The principle of equitable utilization provides equality to both upper and lower riparian states. At the same time, there are provisions not cast as mandatory but 'merely recommend procedures to be followed'.[285]

In addition to the earlier prepared chapters on navigation, timber floating, pollution, and settlement of disputes, two new chapters were agreed on within the Rivers Committee (articles on general issues and on equitable utilization).

280 *Id.*, at 462–463.
281 *Id.*, at 467.
282 *Id.*, at 467–468.
283 *Id.*, at 463.
284 *Id.*
285 *Id.*, at 464.

This meant that the twelve years of work of ILA would be finished at the 52nd ILA Conference with the approval of a complex, coherent set of 37 articles on the uses of the waters of international drainage basins. The articles were grouped into six chapters with one annex concerned with implementation of Article XXXIII. Each article is accompanied by comments. The comments following the articles were intended 'as an explanation and, where necessary, an amplification, by way of inclusion and exclusion' of the text of the articles. Most of the comments reflect the consensus reached by Committee members, but because of certain differences in opinion, the Committee decided that no action be taken and the comments not be proposed for adoption by the Conference. The chapter on timber floating has a brief introduction on the subject. The Rivers Committee Report was adopted unanimously by the Helsinki Conference.

5.2 *Resolution of the Conference*

The principles and rules of international law codified by the Rivers Committee were not regarded as an exhaustive account on the subject. On the contrary, as Manner highlighted, the work of the ILA on codification of certain aspects of this field of international law should continue. Speaking on topics for further study, Dr. Gamal M. Badr (Algeria) suggested the issues of legality of diversion of waters beyond the geographical limits of a drainage basin and the distinction between areas already populated and dependant on the waters of the basin and new areas to be settled and brought under cultivation through the use of the basin waters.[286] Dr. L. J. Bouchez (Netherlands) pointed out that administration of international rivers should be covered by articles, that the community of interest of basin states should be emphasized as the basis for common agreement between them, and that practical implementation of the principle of equitable utilization should be reconsidered regularly in order to prevent disputes in cases of changed circumstances regarding use of water resources.[287] Manner pointed out that, concerning the draft articles, 'without doubt still many details [...] need further study and development'. These included: protection of groundwater; many kinds of hydraulic works, including power production; water supply and irrigation; and special problems of pollution, including pollution of groundwater and coastal areas. Finally, he added, 'the work [of the ILA] now concluded may be regarded as incomplete

286 *Id.*, at 447–448.

287 *Id.*, at 454.

and defective if all these questions concerning international water resources remain unsolved'.[288]

The Helsinki Conference adopted Resolution I, Uses of the Waters of International Rivers,[289] which approved the articles that became known as the Helsinki Rules on the Uses of the Waters of International Rivers. Resolution I also set out several recommendations to the Executive Council, including reconstituting the Rivers Committee as the Committee on International Water Resources Law (known also as the Manner's Committee) and instructing the new committee 'to carry on a programme of codification and study of certain selected aspects of water resources law'. Several topics were listed as illustrative:

> underground waters; the relationship of water to other natural resources; domestic uses of water; hydraulic uses of water including generation of power and irrigation; flood control and siltation; regulation of water flow; detailed rules on the navigation of rivers; and further consideration of the subject of pollution of coastal areas and enclosed areas.[290]

The ILA Executive Council asked the Committee to identify its priority topics. Thus, besides successfully wrapping up 10 years of work by the Rivers Committee and 12 years of endeavours by the ILA, Resolution I established the basis for further work by the ILA in this field of international law. Indeed, the ILA would continue its endeavours over the following 34 years, culminating in a comprehensive, coherent, and consistent body of international water law assembled in one document by the Water Resources Committee, the *Campione Consolidation of the ILA Rules in International Water Resources 1966–1999*.[291]

Part 6: The Helsinki Rules

6.1 *Introductory Note*

The 37 articles of the Helsinki Rules, each accompanied by a commentary, are grouped into the following chapters:
Chapter 1 General (Articles I–III);

288 *Id.*, at 465–466.
289 *Id.*, at xi.
290 *Id.*, para. 3 (ii) and (iii).
291 The ILA London Conference (2000) 'took note' of the Campione Consolidation. ILA, *Report of the 69th Conference* (London, 2000), at 40. The Campione Consolidation is available in the Conference Report, at 835–358.

Chapter 2 Equitable Utilization of the Waters of an International Drainage Basin (Articles IV–VIII);
Chapter 3 Pollution (Articles IX–XI);
Chapter 4 Navigation (Articles XII–XX);
Chapter 5 Timber Floating (Articles XXI–XXV);
Chapter 6 Procedures for the Prevention and Settlement of Disputes (Articles XXVI–XXXVII), with an Annex (five articles) for implementation of Article XXXIII.

A brief overview of the contents of each chapter follows.

6.2 *Chapter on General Provisions*

Article I of the Helsinki Rules clearly defines the scope of implementation of all general rules of international law set forth in all chapters. The geographical area of an international drainage basin is a spatial unit to which the rules on the use of waters apply. These rules will not apply if otherwise provided by agreement between states sharing the basin, or in the case of application of a binding custom between states. The comment attached to the article explains that, under international law, states may enter into agreements on any matter and change the rules of international law, as long as such agreement is not in conflict with basic standards of accepted international conduct.

For a long period before the Helsinki Rules were adopted, the scientific community was well aware of the need to deal with water management issues for the entire river basin in an integrated manner.[292] The Helsinki Rules for the first time offered a set of principles and rules of international law that would enable such an integrated approach, connected solely to a geographic area clearly limited by the boundaries of a natural phenomenon (a watershed) and not by political boundaries (state frontiers).[293] This was a huge step forward

292 There is no need here for investigation of the scientific and practical aspects of the water management philosophy behind, for example, the Tennessee Valley Authority, which has implemented an integrated approach. The sources for such investigation are abundant and readily available to the scientific community. However, it seems useful to mention here Ludwik A. Teclaff, *The River Basin in History and Law* (The Hague: Martinus Nijhoff, 1967) and Report of a Panel of Experts, *Integrated River Basin Development*, revised edition (UN Doc. E/3066/Rev. 1), (New York: United Nations, 1970) [hereinafter UN Panel of Experts].

293 Having said this, the justifiable and clear distinction in the Helsinki Rules from this general approach in two cases must be noted. First, is the case of navigation (naturally, these rules only can be connected to 'rivers and lakes portions which are both navigable and separate and traverse the territories', and not to a drainage basin) and second, is the case of timber floating (the rules of which are connected to 'watercourses' that can be both navigable and non-navigable). Both of these cases are discussed in greater detail

in the development of international water law. Therefore, the Helsinki Rules can be seen as an authoritative and influential legal response to the call for 'systematic and persistent' efforts by international community to tackle 'the magnitude of the obstacles inherent in the whole concept of integrated development of an international river basin'.[294]

In comparison, it should be noted that the IIL Madrid Declaration (1911) pertains to 'international rivers' and lakes 'lying between the territories of more than two States'.[295] The rules set out in the IIL Salzburg Resolution (1961) apply to the 'use of waters which are part of a river or of a watershed extending upon the territory of two or more States'. 'River basin" is mentioned in the recital when 'considering that the economic value of the use of waters' and in Article IX in the recommendation for setting up 'joint organizations'. The IIL Athens Resolution on Pollution of Rivers and Lakes and International Law (1979) uses two terms,—'international rivers and lakes' and 'their basins'. The term 'basin' seems to relate to a 'hydrographic basin',[296] which implies a broader context involving more than just waters. Neither of these terms are clearly defined.

Article II of the Helsinki Rules defines an 'international drainage basin' as a geographical area extending over two or more states that is determined by the watershed limits of the system of waters that flow into a common terminus. Both surface and underground waters are encompassed in this definition, as well as groundwaters connected to surface water of a drainage basin. The comment to Article II clearly states that

> [t]he underground waters constituting a part of the drainage basin described in this article are those that contribute to its principal river, a stream or lake or another common terminus.

Article III contains the definition of a 'basin State', which is a state the territory of which includes a portion of an international drainage basin. This definition

elsewhere in this monograph. However, unlike the term 'navigable river or lake', the Helsinki Rules do not define the term 'watercourse which flows through or between the territories of two or more States'. It is interesting to note that the IIL Madrid Declaration (1911) uses several different terms—'common stream' and 'stream', 'natural watercourse', 'international rivers' and 'international stream'—without defining any them. *See* Salman & Uprety, *supra* note 116, at 18–9.

294 UN Panel of Experts, *supra* note 292, at 39.

295 *See* the Statement of Reasons of the Madrid Declaration.

296 As mentioned in Article IX. In different contexts regarding pollution several terms were used, namely, 'basin', 'the whole basin', 'the entire basin', and 'part of the basin'.

shifted the focus from only surface waters of a drainage basin towards applicability of the rules to connected underground waters. However, the waters of confined aquifers shared by two or more states were left outside of application of the Helsinki Rules.

Groundwaters that are not connected to surface waters of a drainage basin (flowing into a common terminus) are not subject to application of the Helsinki Rules. This lacuna was later addressed by the Manner's Committee, and finally, the ILA adopted the Rules of International Groundwaters (1986). Following the Helsinki Rules framework, four articles set out the rules of international law on groundwater. The waters of an aquifer intersected by the boundary between two or more states were defined as 'international groundwaters', which together with aquifer form an international basin or part thereof.[297] The final, consolidated definition of international drainage basin developed by ILA reads:

1. An international drainage basin is a geographical area extending over two or more States determined by the watershed limits of the system of waters, including surface and groundwater flowing into a common terminus.
2. The water of an aquifer that is intersected by the boundary between two or more States is international groundwater and such an aquifer with its water forms an international basin or part thereof. Those States are basin States whether or not the aquifer and its water form surface waters part of a hydraulic system flowing into a common terminus.
3. As used in these Rules:

   "aquifer" means all underground strata capable of yielding water on a practicable basis, including fissured or fractured rock formations and the structures containing deep, so called "fossil waters";

   "basin State" means a State the territory of which includes a portion of an international drainage basin.[298]

Throughout the Helsinki Rules, the term 'basin State' replaced the common traditional use of the terms 'riparian', 'co-riparian', 'upper riparian', and 'lower riparian'. This new concept enabled inclusion of states whose territories contribute to the waters of an international drainage basin even if they are not 'riparian states'.[299] In the UN Watercourses Convention terminology, the

297 A definition of the term 'aquifer' was provided in a footnote to Article 1 of Rules on International Groundwaters. For exhaustive information, *see* ILA, *Report of the 62nd Conference* (Seoul, 1986), at 21, 235, and particularly Part II of the Committee Report, prepared by Hayton, at 238–274.

298 *The Campione Consolidation*, *supra* note 291, at 835–836.

299 *See* comment to Article III of the Helsinki Rules.

'Watercourse State' is a term denominating a party to the Convention 'in whose territory part of an international watercourse is situated', but, differently from the Helsinki Rules, also includes 'a regional economic integration organization'.[300]

6.3 *Chapter on Equitable Utilization*

Article IV sets out the key principle of international law that recognizes the right of each basin state to an entitlement to a reasonable and equitable share in the beneficial uses of the waters of an international drainage basin within its territory. The Harmon Doctrine, based on the theory of unlimited sovereignty, was clearly abandoned here in favour of equitable sharing of waters with a view to providing the maximum benefit to each basin state to the minimum detriment of each.[301] The concept of beneficial use was defined as a use that is economically and socially valuable.[302]

Article V lists factors that should be considered in determining what is a reasonable and equitable share within the meaning of Article IV. The list is open ('not limited') and other relevant factors also can be considered. The list consists of eleven factors:

- Geography of the drainage basin (including in particular the extent of the drainage area in the territory of each basin state);
- Hydrology of the basin (including in particular the contribution of water by each basin state);
- Climate (affecting the basin);
- Past and existing utilization of waters of the basin;
- Economic and social needs of each basin state;
- Population dependent on the waters in each basin state;
- Comparative cost of alternative means of satisfying the economic and social needs of each basin state;
- Availability of other resources;
- Avoidance of unnecessary waste of waters;
- Practicability of compensation as a mean of adjusting conflicts among uses;
- The degree to which the needs of a basin state may be satisfied without causing substantial injury to a co-basin state.

The weight to be given to each factor is to be determined by its importance in comparison with the importance of other relevant factors. All the factors

300 United Nations Convention on the Law of Non-Navigational Uses of International Watercourses, 21 May 1997, art. 2 (c).

301 *See* comment to Article IV of the Helsinki Rules.

302 For more discussion on the features of a 'beneficial use', *see id.*

relevant are to be considered together and a conclusion in determining what is a reasonable and equitable share of benefits is to be reached on the basis of the whole.

In light of the differences between the meaning of the concepts of 'equitable utilization' and 'reasonable share', this article should be seen as a provision indicating/requiring application of the principle (or standard) of 'reasonable use' inside the concept of equitable utilization. The common law standard of 'reasonable use of water', the origins of which can be traced from the early thirteenth century in England, enables courts to decide ('to measure') whether a use of the waters shared among holders of water rights is reasonable and to what extent. In common law systems (e.g., the eastern US states) its application assumes that each landowner is entitled to withdraw surface water and use it for beneficial purposes as long as such use does not unreasonably interfere with other legitimate uses of riparian landowners. The rule of reasonable use of groundwater (the American rule) allows a landowner to extract groundwater 'as he needs, notwithstanding any adverse effects on neighbouring landowners, if the use is reasonably related to the natural uses of his overlying land'.[303]

The common law water allocation doctrines (riparian natural flow and reasonable use rules, applicable to determination of consumptive surface waters rights, and absolute ownership and American rules, applicable for determination of consumptive rights to percolating groundwater) were considered outmoded and 'neither efficient nor hydrologically sound' enough to reflect the features of and changes in the hydrological cycle that influence the growing needs for allocation of water rights and to protect the water quality. This perception in the late 1960s and early 1970s was an impetus for development of the *Model Water Code* for the State of Florida.[304] The idea was to overcome those common law doctrines in a way that recognizes hydrologic realities by

303 R. C. Ausness, *'The Influence of the Model Water Code on Water Resources Management Policy in Florida'*, 3:1 Journal of Land Use & Environmental Law (1987), 1–32. For more details on the difference between these two principles, their application in common law, and interstate relations regarding shared waters, *see Vermejo River Cases* (*Colorado v. New Mexico* [*Vermejo I*], 459 U.S. 176, 184 [1982] and [*Vermejo II*], 467 U.S. 310 [1984]). With regards to their formulation in international law, the Helsinki Rules, the ILC Draft Articles on the Law of the Non-navigational Uses of International Watercourses (preparatory to the 1997 UN Convention on the Law of International Watercourses), the 1997 UN Watercourses Convention, and the ILA Berlin Rules, *see* M. J. Vick, *'The Law of International Waters: Reasonable Utilization'*, 12:1 Chicago-Kent Journal of International and Comparative Law (2012), 141–178.

304 This code was drafted at the University of Florida (1967–1972) by Franke E. Maloney, J. Scott Morris, and Richard C. Ausness.

establishing an administrative institutional mechanism (a state agency) that would regulate consumptive uses and water pollution. The concept also was intended to institutionalize a comprehensive planning process (with the focus on water supply and water quality issues) and to create a permit system that would enable planning decisions to be operationalized in practice.[305]

The concept of 'reasonable use' (as 'the only measure of riparian rights')[306] in the United States originally was defined by courts. Eventually, the concept was transformed into a form of legislative and governmental control through permitting of uses.[307] One practical adjustment of the reasonable use principle is the concept of 'regulated riparianism'.[308] This concept is based on the government permitting system and reflects three inherent theoretical principles, namely, sharing of waters by riparians on an equitable basis, banning unreasonable interference by any user of a reasonable use by another riparian, and, in case of conflicting uses, requiring that the utility (benefit) of one use must outweigh the gravity of any harm.[309]

In an international context, the standard of reasonable use is applicable to certain behaviour of states in their territories. However, it seems that it would not be possible to expect any transcendence of that standard into any form of supra-state regulatory mechanism that would be mandatory in the absence of an agreement between the states involved. Certainly there is no prospect of imposing an 'international regulatory riparian' (supranational) mechanism binding on basin states without a clear expression of the desire of the states to accept such a mechanism in the form of either an international treaty or arrangement. From this perspective, the formal normative expression of any standard requiring permission from any kind of supranational authority or other interested states can easily be seen as an intrusion of the sovereign rights of basin states. Therefore, a careful legislative formulation of the principle of reasonable use is of the utmost importance. The formulation of Article V of the Helsinki Rules (as read in conjunction with Article IV on

305 Ausness, *supra* note 303, at 13.

306 American Law Institute, '*Restatement of the Law on Torts Second § 850–857 (1939) Reasonableness of the Use of Water, Annex Factors to Determine Reasonable Utilization*', and *Restatement of the Law Second Torts* §§ 841–848 (1979). (St. Paul, MN: American Law Institute Publishers, 1979).

307 Vick, *supra* note 303, at 153.

308 *Id.* The term denominates 'the new system of water law that converted common law riparian systems to the state issued permits' in the Model Water Code developed by the American Society of Civil Engineers (2004).

309 *Id.*, at 151–152.

equitable utilization) seems to be correct in that sense. It did not raise any concerns or doubts along this line.

According to Article VI of the Helsinki Rules, there is no inherent preference of any use or category of uses over any other use or category of uses. Navigation has lost its historical preference over other uses. All uses are now on the same footing and their relations must be examined and determined in each drainage basin individually. The comment to Article VI is clear in that

> no factor has a fixed weight nor will all factors be relevant to all cases. Each factor is given such weight as it merits relative to other factors. And no factor occupies a position of pre-eminence *per se* with respect to any other factor. Further, to be relevant, a factor must aid in the determination or satisfaction of the social and economic needs of the co-basin states.[310]

The Rivers Committee investigated a proposition that the use of water for domestic purposes[311] should succeed navigation as a preferential use, because it would make these uses, which are 'the basis of life', the first to be satisfied. However, no substantial authority for that was found. The Committee was firm in its position that recognizing any artificial preference was unnecessary and that it would be inconsistent with the principle of equitable utilization. Giving such preference in one basin state might lead to the unjust implementation of a development project (in conflict with such domestic uses) of another co-basin state despite there being an equally convenient source of water to satisfy domestic uses. The Committee concluded that, because of the character of domestic uses (the basis of life), 'it would not have difficulty in prevailing on the merits against other uses in an evaluation of the drainage basin'.[312]

In the IIL Salzburg Resolution (1961) the 'right [of one state] to make use of waters' was limited to the 'waters flowing across or bordering its territory', and 'by the rights of use by other States concerned'.[313] In cases of disagreement concerning the rights of use, 'the disagreement shall be settled on the basis of equity'. The respective needs of the states involved shall be taken into consideration, 'as well as any other circumstances relevant to any particular

310 *See* comment to Article V of the Helsinki Rules.

311 Domestic uses were always considered to be a freedom ('freedom of use of water' for personal and domestic purposes) guaranteed by customary water law, not a kind of 'right' that would be permitted by an authority. This freedom originated in Roman Law. In modern times, such a freedom is guaranteed by national laws.

312 *See* comment to Article VI of the Helsinki Rules.

313 Art. II.

case'.[314] In a recital to the Resolution on Pollution of Rivers and Lakes and International Law (Athens, 1979), recalling its Madrid (1911) and Salzburg (1961) resolutions, the IIL expressed its awareness

> of the multiple potential uses of international rivers and lakes and of the common interest in a rational and equitable utilization of such resources through the achievement of a reasonable balance of various interests.

Article VII of the Helsinki Rules provides that a basin state may not be denied the present reasonable use in favour of reservation of a future use for another co-basin state. This article was seen as ensuring the flexibility and future readjustment implicit in the principle of equitable utilization. Once another co-basin state is ready to use water, 'the entire question of equitable utilization of the waters is opened up for review under Article V and the rights and needs of the various States will be considered'.[315]

Article VIII sets out the rules regarding the protection, creation, and termination of an existing use. An existing use may continue until the factors justifying its continuance are outweighed by other factors that lead to the conclusion that the existing use must be modified or terminated in order to accommodate to a competing incompatible use.[316] Determining when an operational use will be deemed an existing use depends on the timing of the initiation of construction directly related to the use. Where there is no construction required, the timing of undertaking comparable acts of actual implementation will be relevant.[317] An existing use continues to be such until the time when it is discontinued with the intention of being abandoned.[318] However, a use shall not be deemed existing if, at the time it became operational, it was incompatible with an already existing reasonable use.[319]

The Manner's Committee scrutinized the provisions concerning legal limits of the use of the waters of international watercourses a few years later. After a careful analysis of the issue, the Committee concluded that the respective articles of the Helsinki Rules do not contain provisions regulating injurious activities resulting from enjoying the rights of basin states to use basin waters.[320] In other words, the Helsinki Rules did not establish the legal limits

314 Art. III.
315 *See* comment to Article VII of the Helsinki Rules.
316 Art. VIII, para. 1.
317 Art. VIII, para. 2 (a).
318 Art. VIII, para. 2 (b).
319 Art. VIII, para. 3.
320 Article X of the Helsinki Rules relates only to substantial injury caused by pollution.

for practical implementation of the equitable utilization principle. The New York Recommendations (1958) contained a provision with such a recommendation. The reason for this lacuna in the Helsinki Rules is not clear. Therefore, in view of developments regarding this issue,[321] the ILA drafted and approved a new Complementary Rule.[322] Article I, Substantial Injury, reads:

> A basin State shall refrain from and prevent acts or omissions within its territory that will cause substantial injury to any co-basin State, provided that the application of the principle of equitable utilization as set forth in Article IV of the Helsinki Rules does not justify an exception in a particular case. Such an exception shall be determined in accordance with Article V of the Helsinki Rules.

In that way, *inter alia*, a clear relationship between the principle of equitable utilization and the duty not to cause substantial injury was established. Duty to prevent acts and omissions that will cause substantial injury is actually one of the factors to be used in the determination of a reasonable and equitable share. This duty pertains to the uses that are not justified by application of the Helsinki Rules principle of equitable utilization (as defined in Article IV). This exception must be ('shall') determined only in the context of relevant factors in accordance with Article V of the Helsinki Rules.[323] This duty of a basin state pertains to both rights and interests of a co-basin state. The term 'substantial injury' was used here instead of the term 'appreciable harm', which was used in the ILC Draft Articles on the Law of the Non-navigational Uses of International Watercourses. At the time, in the ILC Draft Articles, the term appreciable harm reflected the difference ('lesser quality') between the terms 'serious' or 'substantial',[324] a difference that was considered unnecessary in the Helsinki

321 These developments include the work of the Asian-African Legal Committee, particularly its Proposition IV on the Law of International Rivers (1972), Article 3 of the IIL Salzburg Resolution, and the ILC Draft Articles on the Law of the Non-navigational Uses of International Watercourses (ILC Draft Articles) drafted by S. M. Schwebel and J. Evensen (1981, 1983 and 1984).

322 Article I, Substantial Injury, of the Complementary Rules Applicable to International Water Resources, in ILA, *Report of the 62nd Conference* (Seoul, 1986), at 21.

323 *Id.*, '*Report of the Committee*', part III, particularly at 276 and 278.

324 The ILC Draft Articles and the UN Watercourses Convention used the term 'significant'. In the Report of the Sixth Committee (UN Doc. A/51/869 of 11 April 1997) the following statement of understanding was provided for Article 3 (b): 'The term "significant" is not used in this article or elsewhere in the present Convention in the sense of "substantial". What is to be avoided are localized agreements, or agreements concerning a particular project, programme or use, which have a significant adverse effect upon third watercourse States.

Rules.[325] The duty to refrain from activities that might cause substantial injury, as well as exemption from that duty, are subject to application of the equitable utilization principle. Compensation for losses due to infringement of the right to equitable utilization was seen as a means to restore balance.[326] This duty found its final expression in the Campione Consolidation:

> Article 8
>
> A basin State shall refrain from and prevent acts or omissions within its territory that will cause substantial injury to another basin State, provided that the application of the principle of reasonable and equitable utilization set forth in the above Articles does not justify an exception in a particular case.
>
> Article 9
>
> In the case of a breach of a State's international obligations relating to the waters of an international drainage basin, the State shall cease the wrongful conduct and shall pay compensation for the damage resulting therefrom.

With adoption of Complementary Article I (1986), the ILA established a clear relationship between the principles of reasonable and equitable utilization and the duty not to cause substantial injury. The latter duty is one of the factors in the context of reasonable and equitable utilization that has absolute preference. The principle of equitable and reasonable utilization, established in this way as a key guiding principle of international water law, has been widely recognized as an established principle of international customary law. Recently, strong support for the principle of equitable and reasonable utilization came from the Supreme Court of India in the judgment concerning the allocation of waters of the Cauvery River (2018).[327] The Court made extensive reference to the work of the ILA in the field of international water law, particularly with respect to the provisions of the Helsinki Rules and the Campione Consolidation, but also to certain provisions of the Berlin Rules.

In an atmosphere of defeatism, pessimism, and doubt among several influential scholars that the UN Watercourses Convention would never enter into power (as well as some allegations regarding the correctness of some of its

---

While such an effect must be capable of being established by objective evidence and not be trivial in nature, it need not rise to the level of being substantial' (at para. 8).

325 *See supra* note 323, *'Report of the Committee'*, Comment to the Article I, at 280–281.

326 *Id.*, at 282.

327 *See infra* notes 398–400 and accompanying text.

provisions), the ILA decided to undertake an additional measure at the London Conference (2000). An assignment for the Water Resources Committee was approved aimed at, *inter alia*, incorporating international environmental law, international human rights law, and humanitarian law relating to the war and armed conflicts into a new body of law based on the revision of the Helsinki Rules and subsequently adopted rules, as compiled in the Campione Consolidation. The result, the Berlin Rules (2004), were drafted and approved by the ILA in an exceedingly short period of time.

The story of Berlin Rules is another story, and, because of space limitations, will not be dealt with in this monograph. The reference here relates to the relationship between the above discussed principles in the Berlin Rules. The Berlin Rules were an attempt to revise 'water resources law, as many changes had occurred since 1966 and advances had to be integrated and reflected in a comprehensive manner'.[328]

The aim, it seems, was to prevent the Helsinki Rules from remaining 'merely as a footnote to the UN Convention' if they were not revised.[329] An analysis has shown that, contrary to the Helsinki Rules, the final output of International Law Commission, the UN Watercourses Convention (1997), and the judgment of the ICJ in the *Gabčikovo-Nagymaros Project Case* (1997), the Berlin Rules[330] subordinate the principle of equitable utilization to the 'no harm rule' principle.[331] In a dissenting opinion to the ILA Water Resources Committee Report that contained the Berlin Rules, several members of the Committee, found that the Berlin Rules 'strike at the fundamental basis of the Helsinki Rules and subsequent resolutions of the ILA', which 'would abrogate the customary law on equitable utilization as viewed by the ILA since 1966'.[332] Another analysis concluded that the Berlin Rules subjected the

328 *See* discussion of Professor J. W. Dellapenna (Villanova University, United States) at the Water Resources Committee working session in London (28 July 2000). ILA, *Report of the 69th Conference* (London, 2000), at 871.

329 *Id.*

330 Berlin Rules on Water Resources, in ILA, *Report of the 71st Conference* (Berlin, 2004), arts. 12, 13 and 16.

331 Article 12.1 of the Berlin Rules reads, 'Basin States shall in their respective territories manage the waters of an international drainage basin in an equitable and reasonable manner having due regard for the obligation not to cause significant harm to other basin States' and Article 16 reads, 'Basin States, in managing the waters of an international drainage basin, shall refrain from and prevent acts or omissions within their territory that cause significant harm to another basin State having due regard for the right of each basin State to make equitable and reasonable use of the waters'.

332 ILA, *'Dissenting Opinion'* (to the ILA Water Resources Committee Report), ILA, *Report of the 71st Conference* (Berlin, 2004), https://www.internationalwaterlaw.org/documents/intldocs/ILA/ILABerlinRulesDissent2004.pdf.

principles of equitable and reasonable utilization and the obligation to not cause significant harm to each other, making them equal.[333]

> Thus, rather than clarifying the relation between two principles, the Berlin Rules have added to the already existing confusion in this area. It should be clarified that the harm can be quantitative or qualitative or both. The quantitative harm is addressed through the principle of equitable and reasonable utilization, while qualitative harm is addressed through the environmental obligations.[334]

Hence, the Berlin Rules do not contribute to, or even influence, the progressive development of international water law to deal with the emerging problems of sharing and managing shared watercourses, as evidenced by the dissenting opinion of some members of the ILA Water Resources Committee. Indeed, it can be argued further that the Berlin Rules failed to alter, in any way, the cardinal principles set forth by the Helsinki Rules, or to influence international water law in these areas.

6.4 *Chapter on Pollution*

Article IX of the Helsinki Rules defines 'water pollution' as any detrimental change in the natural composition, content, or quality of waters of an international drainage basin caused by human conduct. Changes that are of concern are ones 'that render the water either unusable or less usable for a beneficial use, or other changes that are of a deleterious nature'.[335] The term 'human conduct' refers to both 'failure to act' and 'affirmative actions'. Natural causes of change are not within the scope of the chapter because 'international law takes no cognizance of them'.[336]

In accordance with Article X, paragraph 1 (a), a basin state has a duty ('must'), consistent with the principle of equitable utilization, to prevent any new form of water pollution or any increase of existing water pollution that would cause substantial injury in the territory of a co-basin state. The paragraph contains, under (b), a recommendation to the basin state regarding existing water pollution that causes 'substantial damage' in the territory of a co-basin state. That state 'should' take all reasonable measures to abate existing

333 S. M. A. Salman, *'The Helsinki Rules, the UN Watercourse Convention and the Berlin Rules: Perspectives on International Water Law'*, 23:4 International Journal of Water Resources Development (2007), 625–640, at 637. DOI: 10.1080/07900620701488562.

334 *Id.*

335 *See* comment to Article IX of the Helsinki Rules.

336 *Id.*

pollution to the level that no substantial damage is caused in the territory of a co-basin state. This rule applies to water pollution originating both in the territory of the basin state and outside of its territory the conduct of the state causes the pollution.[337] These rules were identified in and extracted from decisions of international courts and arbitral tribunals, as well as from a number of national court decisions and treaty law. The comment to Article X refers to the *Corfu Channel Case*,[338] the *Lake Lanoux Arbitration*, the *Trail Smelter Arbitration*, as well as several decisions of the US Supreme Court.[339] The opinion of the Supreme Court of Italy was quoted:

> If this [State], in the exercise of its sovereign right is in a position to establish any regime that it deems most appropriate over the watercourse, it cannot escape the international duty [...] to avoid that, as a consequence of such a regime, other (co-riparian) States are deprived of the possibility of utilizing the watercourse for their own needs.[340]

The opinion of the UN Secretary-General was also quoted:

> There has been general recognition of the rule that a State must not permit the use of its territory for purposes injurious to the interests of other States in a manner contrary to international law.[341]

In the context of equitable use of waters, the duty of a state ('should') to take reasonable measures to abate existing pollution in co-basin state, caused by a use that is consistent with the equitable utilization principle is not absolute and does not apply to the state responsible for pollution.[342] The comment to Article X includes a brief discussion about the 'substantiality' of the injury:

---

337 Helsinki Rules, art. X, para. 2.

338 Every state has an obligation 'not to allow knowingly its territory to be used for acts contrary to the rights of other States'. *Corfu Channel Case* (*United Kingdom v. Albania*), [1949] ICJ Rep. 4, at 22.

339 *Missouri v. Illinois*, No. 4 Original, 200 U.S. 496 (1906); *New York v. New Jersey*, No. 2 Original, 256 U.S. 296 (1921); *New Jersey v. City of New York*, No. 17 Original, 283 U.S. 473 (1931).

340 *Société Énergie Électrique v. Campagnia Imprese Elettriche Liguri*, 64 Foro Italiano, I, 1036, 9 Ann. Dig. 120 (Italy Court of Cassation, 1939), at 120.

341 United Nations General Assembly, 'Survey of International Law in Relation to the Work of Codification of the International Law Commission', UN Doc. A/CN.4/1/Rev. 1, 10 February 1949, para. 57, at 36.

342 *See* comment to Article X of the Helsinki Rules.

> Not every injury is substantial. Generally, an injury is considered "substantial" if it materially interferes with or prevents a reasonable use of water.

Article XI, paragraph 1, sets out the applicable rule of international law when a basin state is responsible for substantial injury in the territory of a co-basin state due to violation of the obligation to prevent any new form of water pollution or any increase of existing pollution causing substantial injury.[343] In such cases, the basin state responsible 'shall be required' to cease the wrongful conduct and to compensate the injured co-basin state for the injury caused. Paragraph 2 relates to cases where a basin state fails to take reasonable measures to abate existing pollution.[344] In such cases the state 'shall be required' to promptly enter into negotiations with the injured state, with a view of reaching an equitable solution. This rule is rooted, *inter alia*, in the *Case Concerning the Factory at Chorzów*, where the PCIJ found that violation of international law results in an obligation 'of the offending State to make reparation in an appropriate manner so as to do justice under the circumstances'.[345]

The pollution of waters of an international drainage basin was also on the agenda of the Manner's Committee for a long time (1996–1982). Some 15 years after the approval of the Helsinki Rules, it was apparent that its provisions on pollution were no longer fully sufficient.[346] The Rapporteur of the working group, Bourne, submitted a set of draft articles on water pollution in an international drainage basin, which were adopted by the Committee and approved by the ILA Montreal Conference (1982).[347] This work of the Manner's Committee can be considered an exhaustive endeavour to revise and upgrade the three previously adopted Helsinki Rules provisions on pollution. Eleven articles were developed to supplement and elaborate Articles X and XI of the Helsinki Rules.[348] It is important to note that in these rules, the principle of equitable utilization remained the overriding principle, as it was seen as best promoting the objective of reasonable use of shared natural resources.[349]

343 In accordance with Article X, paragraph 1 (a) of the Helsinki Rules.

344 In accordance with Article X, paragraph 1 (b) of the Helsinki Rules.

345 *See* comment to Article XI of the Helsinki Rules.

346 ILA, *Report of the 60th Conference* (Montreal, 1982), at 532.

347 *See* Conference Resolution No. 12, *id.*, at 13.

348 The essence of the definition of the pollution set out in Article IX has been left unchanged. 'There seems to be no good reasons for departing from it in a set of articles designed merely to bring up-to-date and enlarge upon the provisions of the Helsinki Rules'. ILA, Report of the 60th Conference (Montreal, 1982), at 535.

349 See Bourne's discussion at the Committee Working Session, *id.*, at 549.

Professor B. R. Chauhan (India) supported this approach and the set of new rules:

> [I]t is now a well recognized fact that the contribution of this Committee in evolving and consolidating the concept of "equitable utilization" has produced not only academic clarity but also practical utility in the field of international water law.[350]

Observing the progress in developing legal studies of water pollution since 1972, the Committee noted the multilateral treaties dealing with pollution, the work of UN agencies on development of rules to protect the environment (e.g., the Stockholm Declaration 1972[351] and the work of the United Nations Environment Programme), the statements and recommendations of the Organisation of Economic Co-operation and Development on transfrontier pollution, and the IIL Resolution on the Pollution of Rivers and Lakes and International Law (Athens, 1972). However, it concluded that

> those who would codify and develop this branch of the law still do not find it possible to do more than state a few general principles of law.[352]

6.5 *Chapter on Navigation*

The rules on freedom of navigation, as proposed by the Rivers Committee to the Brussels Conference (1962),[353] were included almost in their entirety in the Helsinki Rules. The rules in this chapter refer to rivers and lakes that are both navigable and separate, or traverse the territories of two or more states.[354] Also, navigable canals are not excluded, despite the fact that they are not expressly mentioned in the Helsinki Rules. A tributary is considered as a separate river for the purpose of this chapter, but if it lies wholly in the territory of one state, it will not fall into the scope of definition of 'navigable river' and this chapter would not apply to it. However, due to such a tributary being part of an international drainage basin, it would be subject to other rules (e.g., on equitable utilization and pollution).

---

350 *Id.*, at 551.

351 Declaration of the United Nations Conference on the Human Environment, (Stockholm, 1972).

352 ILA, *supra* note 346, at 535.

353 *See* Fortuin's third report, *supra* note 244 and accompanying text.

354 Helsinki Rules, art. XII.

A special definition regarding the shared waters was formulated for navigation. Article XII, paragraph 1 of the Helsinki Rules defines a navigable river in terms of an interstate border. In the light of limited territorial sovereignty, the appropriate general rule of international law was identified, which gives equal rights to states sharing streams as a boundary 'to use the boundary waters as an incident to its ownership of a portion of the bed'. At the same time, considering that the Harmon Doctrine does not offer widely accepted principles, the rule of international law was safely identified, which 'gives all states riparian to a river equal rights to make reasonable use of its waters'.[355]

The rules on navigation in this chapter are discussed above. Here it should be added that application of the principles of international law relevant in cases of improvement of natural waterways, which required resolving all issues affecting navigation to be settled by agreement, was omitted from the articles in this chapter. Whereas 'riparian States are constituting a community of interest in everything concerning navigation', consequentially, the duty to cooperate principle applies. This duty is inherent to the principle of reasonable and equitable utilization. Although the Helsinki Rules include navigation as one use, it has no priority over conflicting non-navigational uses.[356]

In an attempt to deal with the issue of such conflicting uses, Manner's Committee addressed the topic of navigation a few years later and drafted several new rules.[357] These rules relate to the procedures that riparian states should use to maintain and improve navigable waterways. As Rapporteur Zurbrügg noted, freedom of navigation imposes on riparian states not only

---

355 J. Lipper, *'Equitable Utilization'*, in A. H. Garretson, R. D. Hayton & C. J. Olmstead (eds.), *The Law of International Drainage Basins* (Dobbs Ferry, NY: Oceana Publications, 1967), at 23–25.

356 *See* Zurbrügg's Preliminary Study, *infra* note 357, *passim.*

357 Navigation was one of the first topics dealt with by the second ILA water committee, the Manner's Committee. *See* the Manner's Committee Progress Report, ILA, *Report of the 53rd Conference* (Buenos Aires, 1968), at 522 and 524. At the meeting of 11 May 1974, the ILA Executive Council appointed Zurbrügg as the Chairman-Rapporteur of the Working Group on Navigation. ILA, *Report of the 56th Conference* (New Delhi, 1974), at xxi. This move followed the position taken by the Committee (at its 1970 meeting in The Hague) on Zurbrügg's *'Preliminary Study on Some Legal Aspects of Maintenance and Improvement of Naturally Navigable Waterways Separating or Traversing Several States'.* Following the Committee requirement set out at a meeting in New York in 1972, Zurbrügg revised the study on the basis of discussion at the Committee meeting in Bonn (April 1973). The revised study was distributed among the members of the Committee before the meeting in Geneva (April 1974). At that meeting the Committee adopted (with some amendments) the report and decided to submit it to the New Delhi Conference (1974). ILA, *Report of the 56th Conference* (New Delhi, 1974), at 114–116. For the final text of the Zurbrügg Report, *see id.*, at 117–128.

a negative requirement, namely, to avoid implementation of measures that obstruct navigation (new bridges, construction projects, wreck ships, etc.), but also a positive duty, which includes undertaking technical measures (e.g., dredging and constructing hydraulic objects) to reduce the harmful effects of erosion and siltation to navigation.[358]

As the result of the work by the Manner's Committee on navigation, the ILA Conference (New Delhi, 1974) added Article XVIII bis to the Helsinki Rules. Paragraph 1 establishes the duty of a riparian state intending to undertake improvement works in its territory to give notice to co-riparian states. Paragraph 2 provides each riparian state with the right to request consultation if navigational uses are likely be affected adversely by these works. Paragraph 3 sets out the rule that in cases when such works are proposed to be undertaken in whole or in part in the territory of other (one or more) co-riparian states, the state proposing the works must obtain the consent of the co-riparian states concerned. In such cases, the co-riparian states are under a duty to negotiate.

6.6 *Chapter on Timber Floating*

The text of the five articles on timber floating as agreed on during the Tokyo Conference (1964) were incorporated as Chapter 5 in the Helsinki Rules with no further changes. A short introduction to the chapter and comments accompany the articles. There are no generally accepted rules of international law regulating floating of timber[359] on international rivers. However, there are factors that support the opinion that floating of timber, except rafts, should be considered a non-navigational use.[360] In his report, Manner proposed five articles[361] that would be applicable to floating timber on watercourses that flow through or between the territories of two or more states when there are no rules of navigation established by applicable law or custom regulating floating or otherwise binding riparian states.[362]

Riparian states of an international watercourse used for navigation have the right to agree whether or not the floating of timber will be permitted on the watercourse and under what conditions.[363] With regards to watercourses

358 Zurbrügg Report, *id.*, at 123.

359 There are different systems of floating timber, namely, floated loosely, fastened together as rafts, or tied in bundles or bundle-rafts. See Manner's report on timber floating, ILA, *Report of the 51st Conference* (Tokyo, 1964), at 169.

360 *Id.*, at 170.

361 The substance of the text of those provisions was not changed, but was technically corrected to harmonize with other articles in the Helsinki Rules.

362 The first article proposed by Manner was adopted as Article XXI of the Helsinki Rules.

363 The second article proposed by Manner was adopted as Article XXII of the Helsinki Rules.

not used for navigation, it is recommended that each riparian state permit co-riparian states to use watercourses and their banks in their territories for floating of timber, including all necessary activities and works of a floating crew.[364] An agreement between interested states should be concluded if a riparian state requires permanent installations to be constructed inside the territory of a co-riparian state, or if there is a need to regulate the water flow.[365] In such cases, the co-riparian states should negotiate with a view to reaching an agreement that would govern the administrative regime of timber floating and, if necessary, establish a joint agency to facilitate all aspects of floating.[366]

As a result of a comprehensive revision and update of several Helsinki Rules by the Complementary Rules Applicable to International Water Resources (1986), Article II was approved, which deals with extra-territorial operations. That article was developed with reference to the IIL Madrid Declaration (1911), the Geneva Convention (1923), and Article XXIV of the Helsinki Rules relating to the floating of timber. If an undertaking of a basin state requires that works or installations or utilization of water resources are to be located in a co-basin state, all related issues are to be determined by agreement, in accordance with the principle of equitable utilization, by means of using the best endeavours of the states concerned to reach a just and reasonable solution. This article fills a gap in this general rule.[367]

Finally, it should be noted that as concerns timber floating, the Helsinki Rules use a specific term instead of the term 'international drainage basin', similar to that used under navigation. This chapter uses the expression 'a watercourse which flows through or between the territories of two or more states'.[368]

6.7 *Chapter on Procedures*

The text of the articles on settlement of disputes formulated and accepted at the Committee meeting in The Hague (1961)[369] were almost in their entirety incorporated into the Helsinki Rules (1966). The two versions of the text differ because of the inclusion of the rules on procedures for the prevention of disputes. The focus was shifted from international river, river system, or watercourse to international drainage basin, and some technical improvements

364 The third article proposed by Manner was adopted as Article XXIII of the Helsinki Rules.
365 The fourth article proposed by Manner was adopted as Article XXIV of the Helsinki Rules.
366 The fifth article proposed by Manner was adopted as Article XXV of the Helsinki Rules.
367 See comment to Article II of the Complementary Rules. ILA, *Report of the 62nd Conference* (Seoul, 1986), at 284–285.
368 *See* Helsinki Rules, art. XXI, and other articles in Chapter 5.
369 The meeting in The Hague was held 1–5 September 1961.

of the text were also made.[370] A substantial change of the new text of the articles in comparison to the Hamburg Recommendations is an explicit recalling of the ILC Model Rules on Arbitral Procedure (1958) in Article X (of the text from The Hague), i.e., Article XXXV of the Helsinki Rules. The annex to the Committee articles, aimed at implementing Article VIII, the Model Rules for Constitution of a Conciliation Commission for the Settlement of a Dispute, was fully incorporated into the Helsinki Rules as an annex in order to implement Article XXXIII of the Helsinki Rules.

Article XXVI set out the scope of Chapter 6, which deals with the prevention and settlement of international disputes regarding legal rights and other interests of basin states and other states. Mention of 'other states' is made because such states may have interests in navigation and may be affected by pollution.[371] The term 'dispute' is used here in its broader meaning to include 'differences' among states concerning certain issues.[372] The articles of this chapter contain only codified rules of customary international law and certain recommendations.[373] In line with the UN Charter, Article XXVII recalls the obligation of states to settle international disputes (which can relate to interpretation of a treaty, any question of international law, or existence of any fact of breaching of an international obligation[374]) by peaceful means, in a manner such that international peace, security, and justice are not endangered. Article XXVII recommends progressive resort to the means of prevention and settlement of disputes set out in Articles XXIX–XXXIV of this chapter. Article XXVIII provides that, in order to prevent and resolve disputes, states have a primary obligation to resort to the means in accordance with binding treaties, but only to the extent provided by such treaties.

With a view to preventing disputes, Article XXIX recommends that each basin state provide relevant and reasonably available information to other basin

---

370 Article I was corrected and reflected in Article XXVI of the Helsinki Rules, Article II corresponds to Article XXVII of the Helsinki Rules, Article III corresponds to the Article XXVIII of the Helsinki Rules, while Article IV was omitted. Article V (1) is the same as Article XXIX (1) of the Helsinki Rules, and Article V (2) corresponds to Article XXX of the Helsinki Rules. Article VI is slightly adjusted to encompass the drainage basin concept, and its paragraphs (2) and (3) exchange places in Article XXXI of the Helsinki Rules. The same corrections are visible in Articles VII–XII, which became Articles XXXII–XXXVII of the Helsinki Rules. Committee members discussed these difference at the Conference in Tokyo in 1964, which led to the text of the provisions being included in the Helsinki Rules. *See* ILA, *Report of the 51st Conference* (Tokyo, 1964), at 147–162.

371 *See* comment to Article XXVI.

372 *See* comment to Article XXVII.

373 *See* comment to Article XXVIII.

374 ICJ Statute, art. 36, para. 2.

states concerning the waters of a drainage basin in its territory, its use, and respective activities. Irrespective of its location in the drainage basin, it is recommended that a state provide to 'any other basin state', whose interests may be substantially affected, notice of any proposed construction or installation that would alter the regime of the basin and cause a dispute. Such notice should include essential facts that will permit the recipient to assess the probable effects of the proposed alteration of the regime of basin. States should be afforded a reasonable period of time for assessing effects and submitting feedback. If notice of such proposed construction or installation is not submitted, in the event of a determination of what is a reasonable and equitable share of the waters, the proposed alteration shall not be given weight 'normally accorded to temporal priority in use' (Article XXIX).

Twenty years later, in 1986, the notification procedures set out in paragraph 2 of Article XXIX were considered 'inadequate and, in the light of recent development of international law, insufficient'.[375] The article on notification and objection, complementary to the Helsinki Rules, was approved.[376] That article sets out several rules, including the general duty to notify (the basin state 'shall')[377] and to provide 'a reasonable period of time, which shall be not less than six months', for the evaluation of the project and to communicate reasoned objections.[378] Where there are no objections, the proposing state may proceed with the proposed project in accordance with the notice.[379] If an objection is submitted, the states concerned 'shall make every effort expeditiously to settle the matter' in accordance with the articles in Chapter 6 of the Helsinki Rules. During the period when 'these efforts are continuing', the proposing state shall not proceed with the project. This rule should be effective if such efforts 'are not unduly protracted'. If they 'become unduly protracted, or an objecting state has refused to have resort to third party procedures for settlement of the remaining differences', the proposing state may proceed with the project in accordance with the notice on its own responsibility.[380] The notice and all other communication between involved states shall be transmitted through appropriate official channels, unless otherwise agreed.[381] These

375 *See* comment to Article III 'Notification and Objection' of the ILA Complementary Rules. ILA, *Report of the 62nd Conference* (Seoul, 1986), at 277 and 286–294.
376 Complementary Rules, art. III. *See id.*, at 286.
377 Complementary Rules, art. III, para. 1.
378 Complementary Rules, art. III, para. 2.
379 Complementary Rules, art. III, para. 3.
380 Complementary Rules, art. III, para. 4.
381 Complementary Rules, art. III, para. 5.

complementary rules were developed in light of actual developments in international law (particularly the work of the ILC), as well as the specific earlier rules adopted by the ILA concerning navigation, regulation, and pollution.[382]

Article XXX of the Helsinki Rules recommends that states involved in a dispute regarding their legal rights and interests seek a solution by negotiation. If a question or dispute arises regarding present or future utilization of waters of a drainage basin, it is recommended that states refer it to a joint agency with a request to the agency to survey the drainage basin and to formulate plans and recommendations 'for the fullest and most efficient use' of its waters in the interest of all involved countries. The joint agency should be instructed to submit its report (in accordance with the assignment conferred) to the authorities of the states concerned. If non-basin states enjoy a right to use waters of a drainage basin in accordance with a treaty, it is recommended that they to be associated with the work of the joint agency, or permitted to appear before the agency (Article XXXI). If the question or dispute is considered by the states concerned to be incapable of resolution through deployment of a joint agency, Article XXXII recommends that the states seek the good offices, or jointly request the mediation of a third state, of a qualified international organization or a qualified person. If all above indicated means fail, Article XXXIII recommends that the states form a commission of inquiry or an *ad hoc* conciliation commission to resolve the dispute. Such a commission should be formed in the manner set forth in the Annex.[383] When a conciliation commission is not formed, or the commission is unable to recommend a solution, or if its recommended solution is not accepted by the states concerned, or in cases

382 In particular, Article 1 on Navigation (New Delhi, 1974), Article 7 on Regulation of the Flow of Water of International Watercourses (Belgrade, 1980), and Article 5 on pollution (Montreal, 1982). For details *see* Part III of the Committee Report, *'Complementary Rules Applicable to International Water Resources'*, in ILA, *Report of the 62nd Conference* (Seoul, 1986), at 275–294.

383 The Annex contains model rules and recommends that the members and president of such a commission would be appointed by the states concerned (Article I). When states cannot agree on these appointments, they are to appoint two members, who in turn would appoint a third member to serve as the president. If this procedure fails, the president would be appointed, on the request of any state concerned, by the president of the ICJ or, if this does not happen, by the UN Secretary-General (Article II). The members of the commission should be persons who, 'by reason of their special competence, are qualified' (Article III). Article IV sets out recommendations regarding replacement of members of the commission. Article V sets out the right of the conciliation commission to determine the place of its meeting and establish its own procedures in the absence of an agreement of the concerned parties.

when an agreement is not otherwise arrived at, Article XXXIV recommends that the states concerned agree to submit their legal disputes to an *ad hoc* tribunal, to a permanent arbitral tribunal, or to the International Court of Justice. If they choose arbitration, it is recommended that they have recourse to the ILC Model Rules on Arbitral Procedure (1958). This implies that the states concerned consider the award to be given as final and that they submit to its execution in good faith (Articles XXXV and XXXVI). The means of settlement set out in this chapter do not prejudice the use of means of settlement recommended to or required of members of regional arrangements, agencies or other international organizations (Article XXXVII).

Thus, the Helsinki Rules cover a wide array of issues concerning drainage basins and have been updated, up-graded and, finally, consolidated with other rules approved by the ILA. The result is an authoritative set of principles and rules that have influenced and made a major contribution to international water law, as discussed in the concluding part of this monograph.

Part 7: The Influence of the Helsinki Rules

7.1 *Outreach of the Rules across the Globe*

Following the approval of the Helsinki Rules by the Conference (on 20 August 1966), the Full Council of ILA issued a notice to the press at Helsinki announcing that

> [t]he general codification of the law of international rivers received the approval of the International Law Association at the Closing Session of its Helsinki Conference, and in honour of the city in which the Conference was meeting it was decided to entitle this Code the 'Helsinki Rules on the Uses of the Waters of International Rivers.' The Rules cover such subjects as the definition of an international drainage-basin, the equitable sharing of the benefits of international rivers, pollution, navigation, timber-floating and the settlement of disputes concerning some twenty international rivers.
>
> The thirty-six members of the Committee drafting the Rules include experts on water law from both up-stream and down-stream riparians. The preparation of the Helsinki Rules entailed reconciliation of the not infrequently conflicting interests of these upper and lower riparians. The most important governing principle of the codification is the rule that 'Each basin State is entitled to a reasonable and equitable share in the beneficial uses of the waters of an international drainage basin.' This rule

> entails the rejection of the notion that an upper riparian State has an unfettered sovereign right to exploit an international river.[384]

With that notice, the Helsinki Rules entered the realm of international law and were soon widely accepted as reliable legal tools for the prevention and peaceful resolution of disputes regarding international water resources. India embraced the Helsinki Rules. In the work of the sub-committee on the law relating to international rivers of the Asian-African Legal Consultative Committee (AALCC) India persistently advocated that the Helsinki Rules be accepted as the basis for the sub-Committee studies.[385] At the April 1970 meeting in Rome, the Manner's Committee was informed that the Government of Argentina had accepted the Helsinki Rules. In its Second Progress Report, the Committee:

> [T]akes note of the official position taken by the Government of Argentina, which endorses the Helsinki Rules as the basis for its international water policy and which the Committee hopes will stimulate other States to take similar steps of recognition and application of the Helsinki Rules.[386]

Indeed, 'the Helsinki Rules obviously constitute a monumental work. They have had a major impact upon development of the law of international watercourses'.[387] As noted by one leading expert in the field, the Helsinki Rules 'were soon accepted by the international community as customary international law'.[388] In 1975, the Mekong Committee member states (Cambodia, Laos, Thailand and Vietnam) adopted a Joint Declaration of Principles for Utilization of the Waters of the Lower Mekong Basin.[389] These principles 'were fashioned' on the Helsinki Rules, while the provisions on factors listed in Article V of the

384 ILA, *Report of the 52nd Conference* (Helsinki, 1966), at vii–viii.

385 Asian-African Legal Consultative Committee, *Report of the 11th Session* (Accra, 1970), at 244. The sub-Committee agreed on a Draft Proposition on the Law of International Rivers prepared by Mr. K. Uchida (Japan), which was completed under the clear influence of the Helsinki Rules. *See* AALCC *Report of the 12th Session* (Colombo, 1971), at 52–58. (In 2001, the name of the Committee was changed to Asian-African Legal Consultative Organization).

386 Submitted to the 46th ILA Conference (The Hague, 1970).

387 S. McCaffrey, *The Law of International Watercourses Non-Navigational Uses* (Oxford: Oxford University Press (2001), at 321. McCaffrey was the Special Rapporteur for the International Law Commission's work on the law of the non-navigational uses of international watercourses (1985–1991).

388 Bourne, *supra* note 28, at 282.

389 Vientiane, 31 January 1975, http://gis.nacse.org/tfdd/tfdddocs/374ENG.pdf.

Helsinki Rules, were 'reproduced in the Declaration word for word'.[390] In 1973, the sub-committee of AALCC adopted the principle of reasonable and equitable share and, to a large extent, the factors specified in the Helsinki Rules for determining such a share.[391] The Protocol on Shared Watercourse System in the Southern African Development Community (1995) made a clear reference to the Helsinki Rules and borrowed heavily from the Rules.[392]

Bangladesh decided in 1976 to address the United Nations regarding its dispute with India concerning the Farakka Barrage on the River Ganges. The principle of reasonable and equitable share in the beneficial use of waters of an international drainage basin and factors to be used for determination of such a share, as stated in the Helsinki Rules, were referred to by both states. Notwithstanding the fact that this dispute was not resolved through the political channels of the UN, both parties relied on the Helsinki Rules as well as the broader framework of Principle 21 of the Stockholm Declaration of the UN Conference on the Human Environment, which is further evidence of the worldwide acceptance of the Helsinki Rules.[393] The Helsinki Rules also influenced acceptance of certain rules regulating bilateral[394] or regional[395] relations concerning shared waters.

The most recent extensive reference to and elaboration of the Helsinki Rules[396] is found in the judgment of the Supreme Court of India[397] in the case

---

390 Bourne, *supra* note 28.

391 *See* Salman & Uprety, *supra* note 116, at 21–22.

392 For details *see* Revised Protocol on Shared Watercourses (2000), https://www.sadc.int/documents-publications/show/1975.

393 For more details *see* Salman & Uprety, *supra* note 116, at 142–148, particularly at 146.

394 For details and references *see id.*, at 21–22.

395 *See*, e.g., Articles 7 and 9 (regulating the principle of reasonable and equitable utilization and duty to prevent causing significant harm) of the Framework Agreement on the Sava River Basin (2002), http://www.savacommission.org/dms/docs/dokumenti/documents_publications/basic_documents/fasrb.pdf.

396 The case elaborated on several key rules concerning international river basins, including groundwater (through application of the Campione Consolidation provision regarding confined aquifers, i.e., 'fossil waters'), equitable utilization, factors determining equitable utilization, and the duty not to cause substantial injury. The Harmon Doctrine was decisively abandoned.

397 The 465-page verdict in this 140-year long dispute was delivered by Chief Justice Dipak Misra and Justices Amitava Roy and A. M. Khanwilkar. *See Karnataka v. Tamil Nadu* (Civil Appeal No. 2453 of 2007), *Kerala v. Tamil Nadu* (Civil Appeal No. 2454 of 2007) and *Tamil Nadu v. Karnataka* (Civil Appeal No. 2455 of 2007), Judgement (16 February 2018), https://www.thehinducentre.com/multimedia/archive/03225/11993_2007_Judgeme_3225112a.pdf. For a thorough review of the dispute, *see* A. Ranjan, *'The Cauvery Water Disputes in India'*, Institute of South Asian Studies, National University of Singapore Working Paper

of interstate disputes regarding the Cauvery River.[398] Like the US Supreme Court in the *Wyoming v. Colorado Case* (1922), the Supreme Court of India made a 'mass allocation' of waters.[399] The decision was based, *inter alia*, on the recognition that

> being in a state of flow, no State can claim exclusive ownership of such waters or assert a prescriptive right so as to deprive the other States of their equitable share. [...] [T]he right to flowing water is well settled to be a right incident to property in the land and is a right *publici juris* of such character, that while it is common and equal to all through whose land it runs and no one can obstruct or divert it, yet as one of the beneficial gifts of Nature, each beneficiary has a right to just and reasonable use of it. [...] [T]he acknowledged principle of distribution and allocation of waters between the riparian States has to be done on the basis of their equitable share, however contingent on the facts of each case.[400]

In the search for the legal rules that would serve as the ground for its decision, the Court found that

> [t]he common thread decipherable from these Rules [Helsinki Rules, Campione Consolidation, and Berlin Rules[401]] is the universal acknowledgement of the principle of equitable utilization as an effective and workable tool for the management of waters of an international drainage basin.[402]

No. 293 (2018), https://www.isas.nus.edu.sg/wp-content/uploads/2018/04/ISAS-Working-Papers-No.-293-The-Cauvery-River-Water-Dispute-in-India.pdf.

398 The case comprised three disputes, *id.*, namely, *Karnataka v. Tamil Nadu*, *Kerala v. Tamil Nadu*, and *Tamil Nadu v. Karnataka*.

399 The allocation was expressed in the 'thousand millions of square feet', with the total available volume of 740 allocated as follows: 284.75 to the State of Kerala (an additional 14.75 to the earlier volume of 270); 404.25 to the State of Tamil Nadu (14.75 less than the earlier volume of 419), with recognition of its right to use the groundwater, as a kind of compensation for its diminishing volume allocation from surface waters; 7 to the Puducherry area; 10 for environmental protection; and 1,000 to 'inevitable escapages into the sea'. Judgment, *supra* note 397, at 448–449.

400 *Id.*, at 403–404.

401 In this regard, the Berlin Rules were referred to as 'reiterating in essence the Rules as prescribed by the Helsinki Rules'. *Id.*, at 411.

402 *Id.*, at 412.

Explaining the significance of the allocation of the basin waters for drinking and other domestic uses in the city of Bangaluru [Bangalore], the Supreme Court stated:

> It will be inconceivable to have an artificial boundary and deny the population the primary need of drinking water. We [the bench] hold so in the special features of the case keeping in view the global status the city [Bengaluru] has attained and further appreciating the doctrine of equitable proportionality on the bedrock of pressing human needs.[403]

In the view of the Court, the 'international drainage basin concept *per se*' contains 'some identifiable flexibility' such

> that in an exigent fact situation the basin need not be rigorously confined to the area immediately abutting it in a given state but depending on the situational geography may include other areas of the state concerned entitled to the benefit of the basin.[404]

In this way the possibility of 'inter-basin transfers' of water was taken into consideration. The National Water Policy (2002) of India[405] was the policy framework for this approach, and the Court found that

> [i]t is worthy to note that it significantly underlines that water starved areas ought to be serviced by transfer from one river basin to another based on national perspective after taking into account the needs of such areas/basins. Drinking water has been assigned the highest priority in the category of uses.[406]

This is exactly the same idea that was advocated by both Bourne and Andrassy at the meeting of the Rivers Committee in New York (1958) and by Andrassy at the IIL meetings during the drafting of the Salzburg Resolution (1961). Years later, in his analysis of the 'drainage basin approach', Bourne confirmed that there is room for this approach in both the Helsinki Rules

403 *Id.*, at 442–443. The Court here recalled Article 14 of the Berlin Rules, which requires when determining the equitable and reasonable use, water first be allocated to satisfy vital human needs (*id.*, at 412).

404 *Id.*, at 407.

405 Government of India, *'National Water Policy'*, Ministry of Water Resources (New Delhi, 2002), http://nwm.gov.in/sites/default/files/nwp20025617515534.pdf.

406 Judgment, *supra* note 397, at 415.

(1967) and the Salzburg Resolution (1961). Bourne's broader view is worthy of a quotation *in extenso*:

> [T]he legal right of states to take this broader view and to engage in comprehensive regional planning, even when an international drainage basin is involved, is supported by the judicial decisions [...]. It is also supported by the Helsinki Rules, Article v of which [...] expressly requires all relevant factors, including extra-basin factors to be taken into account, and by the 1961 Salzburg Resolution, Article 2 of which provides that the 'respective needs, as well as of other pertinent circumstances', should be considered; although these documents do not expressly confer the right to utilize water outside of its basin, their whole tenor and background show that states do have that right in certain circumstances. [...] The argument against the juridical unity of a drainage basin and in favour of a rule that would allow a comprehensive regional, if not continental, approach to water resources development seems overwhelming.[407]

The judgment of the Supreme Court of India in disputes (civil appeals) regarding the waters of Cauvery River shows how, in resolving difficult problems/conflicts based on differing views on the right to use such waters, the principles and rules identified by an authoritative international non-governmental organization like the ILA, as customary international law, have successfully served their purpose. This is even the case when, and in spite of, its own rules (Helsinki Rules) have been considered 'revised' and 'superseded' by other rules (in this case, the Berlin Rules) developed with the ambition 'to provide a clear, cogent and coherent statement of the customary international law').[408]

7.2 *The Influence of the Rules on the Work of the United Nations*

During the 1940s and 1950s, it was a common perception that international law on international rivers was lagging behind the development needs (necessities) of riparian states and adequate engineering responses to such necessities. The call of UN Secretary-General (1946–1953), Trygve Lie in 1953[409] for 'someone outside' the UN, a 'non-profit, non-governmental agency' to 'interest itself' in developing procedures that would enable states to determine 'what water was whose',[410] was followed by the Secretary-General's report

407 Bourne, *supra* note 28, at 21.
408 *See supra* note 3.
409 *See supra* note 71 and accompanying text.
410 *Id.*

entitled '*Development and Utilization of Water Resources*'[411] and the adoption of a new ECOSOC resolution.[412] ECOSOC Resolution 599 (XXI) of 3 May 1956 reflects well the situation at that time. By that resolution the UN Secretary-General was asked, among other things, 'to constitute a panel of world-renowned experts for reviewing [...] the administrative, economic and social implications of integrated river-basin development, and for advising on the proper action including, if they deem advisable, the convening of an international conference [...]'. Responding to the request, the Panel of Experts was formed and delivered its report '*Integrated River Basin Development*' in late 1957.[413] This report specifically dealt with the 'inadequacy of relevant international law' for 'success of a plan of international basin development', recognizing that

> [f]or many years legal minds have been directing their efforts towards the formulation and systematization of legal principles applicable to users of international rivers, and much attention is being given to such principles at present by the International Law Association and the Institut de droit international.[414]

Concerning the known on-going disputes regarding 'international streams', it was pointed out in the Report that

> the lack of accepted international law on the uses of these streams present a major obstacle in the settlement of differences, with the result that progress in development is often held up for years to the detriment not only of the countries concerned but of the economy of the world in general.[415]

The first edition of the Panel of Experts Report quoted in full the Dubrovnik Draft Statement of Principles with a note that the Statement 'affords a sound

---

411 UN Doc. E/2603 (May 1954).

412 ECOSOC, Resolution 533 (XVIII) International Co-operation with Respect to Water Resource Development (2 August 1954). This resolution, *inter alia*, requested that the UN Secretary-General consult 'with interested non-governmental organizations on ways and means of achieving' the objective that was defined as 'strengthening international technical co-operation in water matters and improving the co-ordination of the related activities of all concerned'.

413 The report was the outcome of two meetings convened in New York in 1957 and was delivered 23 November 1957. A revised edition was published in 1970. *See* UN Panel of Experts, *supra* note 292.

414 *Id.*, at 34.

415 *Id.*, at 44.

basic philosophy for planning and executing a project for integrated river development in an international river basin'. The fifth principle was seen as to be 'useful in furnishing a guide for the solution of disputes with respect to the use of such waters, recognizing as it does the pertinence of all equitable and historical circumstances in the resolution of such disputes'.[416] In the second, revised edition of the Report (1970), the Helsinki Rules were reprinted in an annex.[417] The continued interest in utilization of international fresh water resources at the UN and its agencies,[418] which began in the late 1940s, has kept the issue high on their agendas. Actually, that interest never stopped and has continued to grow over the ensuing decades.

However, at the same time, the International Law Commission was unwilling to put on its agenda the issue of codification of the law applicable to the use of waters of international rivers, considering it to be premature.[419] Yet, the United Nations General Assembly (UNGA) Resolution 1401 (XIV), adopted at its plenary meeting on 21 November 1959, focussed on 'preliminary studies on the legal problems relating to utilization and use of international rivers with a view to determining whether the subject is appropriate for codification'. The result was the well-known report by the UN Secretary-General entitled '*Legal Problems Relating to the Utilization and Use of International Rivers*' (1963).[420] It is an interesting coincidence that Dr. Trygve Lie, who was in the middle of UN activities aimed at searching for viable international law solutions following the request of ECOSOC Resolution No. 346 (XII) of 9 March 1951 concerning international co-operation on water control and utilization, was the Officer of the Executive Council of the ILA as the Honorary Vice-President during the entire period of development of the Helsinki Rules. However, other agencies were also interested in the work of the ILA. Bourne notes that the Rivers Committee initially had eight members (including the chairman); at the end of its tenure the Committee was composed of 36 members and five alternates. Governments involved in water disputes 'were concerned lest the outcome of the Committee's deliberations would prejudice their bargaining positions', which 'was reflected not only in rapid

416 *Id.*, at 35.

417 *Id.*, at 78–80.

418 These agencies include ECOSOC, the International Bank for Reconstruction and Development, UNECE, FAO, World Health Organization, World Maritime Organization and UNESCO.

419 *See* Berber's letter to Eagleton dated 4 October 1957, in World Bank, Folder ID: 1787921, *supra* note 71, at 7.

420 UN Secretary-General Report, *supra* note 40.

increase of in the size of the Committee but also in the individuals who became its members'.[421]

This focus of the UN on international waters led to Resolution 2669 (XXV), which was adopted on 8 December 1970. In this resolution, the UNGA noted the work carried out by international governmental and non-governmental organizations with the aim of 'further development and codification of the law of international watercourses'. Convinced of the necessity to promote 'the work on the progressive development and codification of the law of international watercourses',[422] the UNGA recommended that the ILC 'take up the study of the law of the non-navigational uses of international watercourses with a view to its progressive development and codification'. The UNGA also requested that the UN Secretary-General continue to study this issue and prepare a supplementary report 'taking into account the recent application in State practice and international adjudication of the law of international watercourses, and also intergovernmental and non-governmental studies of this matter'. Pursuant to this resolution, the Secretary-General submitted his Supplementary Report in 1974.[423]

As a delegate of the Government of Finland, Manner[424] requested by a *note verbale* that the UNGA include on its agenda of the twenty-fifth session (1970) an item entitled 'Progressive development and codification of the rules of international law relating to international watercourses'.[425] An attached explanatory memorandum proposed that the International Law Commission 'consider using the Helsinki Rules as a model for its work' and, *inter alia*, that the

> United Nations should further the progressive development and codification of the rules of international law relating to international watercourses, including international drainage basins, and that the General Assembly should take the preliminary action necessary for the attainment of that goal.[426]

421 For more details, *see* Bourne, *supra* note 28, at 235–236.

422 In accordance with Article 13 of the UN Charter.

423 Supplementary Report *'Legal problems relating to the non-navigational uses of international watercourses'*, UN Doc. No. A/CN.4/274, 25 March 1974., YbILC, 1974, Vol. II, Part Two, at 265–366.

424 *Id.*, at 271–272. *See also*, McCaffrey, *supra* note 387, at 321–322.

425 *Official Records of General Assembly, 25th Session, Annexes*, agenda item 91, UN Doc. A/7991 (24 April 1970).

426 Supplementary Report, *supra* note 423, at 271.

The item was included on the agenda and referred to the Sixth Committee for its consideration and report.[427] During the discussion at the Sixth Committee some representatives 'felt that specific mention should be made of the "Helsinki Rules" adopted by the International Law Association' while others 'expressed the view that reference should also be made to the resolution entitled "Utilization of Non-Maritime International Waters (Except for Navigation)" adopted by the Institute of International Law (1961)'.[428] Due to the contrary views expressed (i.e., 'political considerations'),

> [i]t was agreed in the Sixth Committee that intergovernmental and non-governmental studies on the subject, especially those which are of a recent date, should be taken into account by the International Law Commission in its consideration of the topic.[429]

Although the Helsinki Rules were not mentioned here directly, McCaffrey points out that 'it is clear that the Helsinki Rules are, in a very real sense, important precursors of the ILC's draft articles and thus of the UN Watercourses Convention'.[430]

The global efforts of the UN in this field of international law ultimately led to the signing of the UN Watercourses Convention (1997) and to the adoption of the ILC Draft Articles on the Law of Transboundary Aquifers (2008)[431] and the UNGA resolution on the human right to water and sanitation.[432] It should not be forgotten that these UN activities recognized the extensive work of the ILA in this field of international law. For its part, the ILA always took special care to make its results available to the UN and other international organizations engaged in resolving difficult and long-standing problems concerning the use of international watercourses.

It would require another study to highlight in detail all the connections between the Helsinki Rules and other ILA recommendations and supplementary and complementary rules, and the work on the law on non-navigational uses

---

427 On 18 September 1970. *Id.*

428 *Id.*

429 *Id.*

430 McCaffrey, *supra* note 387, *Id.*

431 The document has been submitted to UNGA as a part of the ILC Sixtieth Session Report, in 2008 covering the work of that session. The report with commentaries on the draft articles appears in the *Official Records of the General Assembly, Sixty-third Session*, Supplement No. 10 (UN Doc. A/63/10), http://legal.un.org/ilc/texts/instruments/english/draft_articles/8_5_2008.pdf.

432 'The human right to water and sanitation', adopted on 28 July 2010, UN Doc. A/RES/64/292 (3 August 2010).

at the UN and the results achieved. Still, several most important comparative aspects should be mentioned here. The drainage basin approach is the first. Differently from the ILA rules, the UN Watercourses Convention (1997) uses the term 'international watercourse' to denominate a similar notion using definitions of two specific elements:

> "Watercourse" means a system of surface waters and groundwaters constituting by virtue of their physical relationship a unitary whole and normally flowing into a common terminus;
>
> "International watercourse" means a watercourse, parts of which are situated in different States.[433]

This definition encompasses both the surface and groundwater. There are differences when compared with the definition of an 'international drainage basin' in the Helsinki Rules:

> An international drainage basin is a geographical area extending over two or more States determined by the watershed limits of the system of waters, including surface and underground waters flowing into a common terminus.[434]

However, there are obvious similarities in the contents and scope of these two definitions. Even the same lacuna concerning confined transboundary aquifers in the Helsinki Rules was identified by ILC concerning the scope of the UN Watercourses Convention (1997). The ILA dealt with this lacuna with the approval of the Rules on International Groundwaters (1986);[435] the ILC adopted a set of articles on the law of transboundary aquifers in 2008 to fill the gap.[436]

The principle of reasonable and equitable utilization is the basic principle for determination of 'what water is whose' in both the Helsinki Rules and UN Watercourses Convention. The factors to be used for determination of

---

433 UN Watercourses Convention, art., definitions (a) and (b).

434 Helsinki Rules, art. II.

435 *See* ILA, *Report of the 62nd Conference* Seoul, 1986), at 251. The consolidated definition of 'international drainage basin' was discussed above in the Part Six, 'Chapter on General Provisions'.

436 *Supra* note 431. In the search for providing guidance to governments concerning bilateral or regional agreements and arrangements regulating proper management of transboundary aquifers, the UNGA adopted several resolutions concerning the ILC Draft Articles (UN Docs. A/RES/66/104, 13 January 2012; A/RES/68/118, 16 December 2013; and A/RES/71/150, 20 December 2016).

a reasonable and equitable use are in their substance only slightly different in the two documents. In a comparative analysis, Salman and Uprety found that the

> only major difference is that factor (j) of the Helsinki Rules on "practicability of compensation to one more of the co-basin States as a means of adjusting conflicts among uses" does not have an equivalent in the factors specified in the UN Convention. This is perhaps due to the fact that international trade in water may still be an anathema for most of the developing countries.[437]

Yet, the possibility to apply such or a similar factor, or the factor that would, for example, relate to preserving sustainability of a water (or water-dependent) ecosystem, still can be applied in the context of the UN Watercourses Convention, because the list of factors is open and can be broadened. In that way the Convention, following the concept of the Helsinki Rules, provides the necessary flexibility in determining what an equitable and reasonable utilization is in a particular case. Therefore, it is also possible to include factors reflecting, for example, the binding commitments of basin states concerning preservation, protection, and improvement of the environment of an 'international watercourse' (as defined by the UN Watercourses Convention) or a 'drainage basin' (as defined by the Helsinki Rules) or a 'river/lake basin' (or maybe only a 'catchment area'). A similar argument could be made as regards the judgment of the Supreme Court of India discussed above in the context of the principle of equitable and reasonable share. Also, a precautionary approach in a particular situation (in terms and scope, which the states concerned are jointly committed to) could be added to the list and considered as one of the factors in both the Helsinki Rules and the UN Watercourses Convention.

The relationship between the principles of equitable and reasonable utilization and the duty not to cause significant harm/no harm is the same: the main principle is that of equitable and reasonable utilization. By subjugating the obligation not to cause significant harm to the principle of equitable utilization,[438] the UN Watercourses Convention (notwithstanding the difference in the meaning of the term 'obligation not to cause significant harm') followed the same course as the ILA, or more accurately, the Helsinki Rules (as

---

437 Salman & Uprety, *supra* note 116, at 28.

438 For an analysis of these two principles in the Convention, *see* S. Salman, *'Entry into Force of the UN Watercourses Convention—Why should it Matter?'*, 31:1 International Journal of Water Resources Development (2015), 4–16. DOI: 10.1080/07900627.2014.952072.

amended by Article I of the Complementary Rules and finally shaped by the Campione Consolidation).

The relationship between two established principles of international customary law, the principle of equitable and reasonable utilization and the duty to avoid significant harm, as established by the UN Watercourses Convention (following the approach of the Helsinki Rules) were upheld in the ICJ judgment in the *Gabčikovo-Nagymaros Project Case* (1997). The Court recalled in that judgment its advisory opinion *Legality of the Threat or Use of Nuclear Weapons*,[439] which stressed 'the great significance that it attaches to respect for the environment, not only for States but also for the whole mankind'.

> [T]he environment is not an abstraction but represents the living space, the quality of life and the very health of human beings, including generations unborn. The existence of the general obligation of States to ensure that activities within their jurisdiction and control respect the environment of other States or of areas beyond national control is now part of the corpus of international law relating to environment.[440]

The ICJ recalled also the PCIJ judgment in the *River Oder Case*, specifically the theory of community of interest in a (navigable) river, which provides 'the perfect equality of interest of all riparian States in the use of the whole course of the river and the exclusion of any preferential privilege of any one riparian State in relation to others'.[441] Furthermore,

> modern development of international law has strengthened this principle for non-navigational uses of international watercourses as well, as evidenced by the adoption of the Convention of 21 May 1997 on the Law of the Non-navigational Uses of International Watercourses by United Nations General Assembly.

The Court also found

> that Czechoslovakia, by unilaterally assuming control of a shared resource, and thereby depriving Hungary of its right to an equitable and

439 Advisory Opinion of 8 July 1996 General List No. 95, *ICJ Reports 1996*, at 241–242, para. 29.

440 *Gabčikovo-Nagymaros Project (Hungary/Slovakia)*, Judgment, *ICJ Reports 1997*, at 38, para. 53.

441 *Territorial Jurisdiction of the International Commission of the River Oder*, Judgment No. 16, 1929, PCIJ Series A, No. 23, paragraph [74], at 27.

> reasonable share of the natural resource of the Danube [...] failed to respect the proportionality which is required by international law.[442]

An analysis by Professor Attila Tanzi[443] of the relationship between the UNECE Convention on the Protection and Use of Transboundary Watercourses and International Lakes (Helsinki, 1992) (UNECE Water Convention) and the UN Watercourses Convention (1997), found that

> difference between the two instruments under review concerns their approach to the substantive principles, on the one hand, and to the procedural rules, on the other. [...] [T]he difference between the two texts appears to be one of emphasis and detail, rather than one leading to incompatibility. [...] [T]here is no need to look for the differences between the two Conventions in order to argue for their mutual compatibility.[444] [...]
>
> [D]ifferences between the two Conventions with regard to specific rules on the same subject-matter are hardly ever a matter of conflicting prescriptions, but one of more, or less, stringency or detailed character of such prescriptions. Therefore, it would not be appropriate to consider the relation between the two instruments as one of derogation of the later one from the former under the rule *lex posterior derogat priori*.[445]

The clear requirement in the UNECE Water Convention ('the Parties shall') to 'ensure that transboundary waters are used in a reasonable and equitable way',[446] and the obligation to take into account the transboundary character of their activities, 'which cause or are likely to cause transboundary impact',[447] reflect the core principles of the Helsinki Rules. If such view is justifiable, the implications would be important and far-reaching as noted by Tanzi:

> [F]rom a contextual interpretation of the term "watercourse" in conjunction with other relevant provisions of the UN [Watercourse] Convention,

442 *Gabčikovo-Nagymaros Project Case*, *supra* note 440, at 42, para. 85.

443 *See* A. Tanzi, *The Relationship between the 1992 UNECE Convention on the Protection and Use of Transboundary Watercourses and International Lakes and the 1997 UN Convention on the Law of the Non Navigational Uses of International Watercourses: Report of the UNECE Task Force on Legal and Administrative Aspects* (Geneva, 2000), http://www.unece.org/fileadmin/DAM/env/water/publications/documents/conventiontotal_Eng_final.pdf.

444 *Id.*, at 4.

445 *Id.*, at 36–37.

446 Convention on the Protection and Use of Transboundary Watercourses and International Lakes, Helsinki, 17 March 1992, art. 2, para. 2 (c).

447 *Id.*

> one may reach the conclusion that the drainage basin area can well fall under the purview of its rules, also on account of an ecosystemic approach to the issue, in line with the [UNECE Water] Convention.[448]

In other words, a conceptual analysis of international water law would show that the Helsinki Rules are always the ultimate source of normatively expressed ideas that are broad enough to encompass ecological or ecosystem concerns and to express environmental commitments of basin states. This is particularly the case in their updated and revised form, as expressed in the Campione Consolidation.

These are some, perhaps the most notable (but in no way exhaustive) examples of the different roles that the Helsinki Rules has played, and continues to play, in fulfilling its mission as defined by the Rivers Committee in the early 1950s. As a set of rules, they appear to be 'the fruits of experience' that are 'ripe for codification'.[449] The Rules are a lasting legacy of the ILA, which continue to serve in international community as a source of ideas in 'preparation of a model bilateral treaty, regional arrangement, administrative and technical assistance by United Nations and other international organisations or in disputes settlement'.[450] The legacy is of a non-governmental organization that is fully incorporated into the complex picture of the international law of the twenty-first century.

Conclusion

When I accepted the task to undertake research regarding the Helsinki Rules, more than a half a century after their approval, and to submit the results of the research in this monograph, I wanted to do what was not possible some two decades ago during preparation of the book *International Law of Water Resources: Contribution of the International Law Association (1954–2000)*.[451] In it, I sought to accurately reflect the current rules of international law governing waters of international drainage basins as expressed in the 'black letters' of the articles approved by ILA, with accompanying comments. The articles and

448 Tanzi, *supra* note 443, at 5.

449 Smith, *supra* note 28, at 158.

450 *See* Rao, *supra* note 145.

451 S. Bogdanović, *International Law of Water Resources: Contribution of the International Law Association (1954–2000)*, (London/The Hague/Boston: Kluwer Law International, 2001).

comments were compiled and published together with a limited amount of other pertinent information.

This journey into the history of the ILA and the origins of the Helsinki Rules has shown that the work of the Rivers Committee, which studied the international law applicable to shared watercourses, was a lasting and consistent endeavour. Twelve years of focussed study culminated in 1996 in a historical point in international water law with the approval of the soon to be widely accepted and influential Helsinki Rules. Appearing after World War II, the Helsinki Rules filled a huge gap in international peace and international law, namely, the lack of universally recognized and accepted principles and rules of customary international law applicable to the use of shared waters. That deficiency in law was identified in the global system of United Nations as an obstacle for implementation of technically available and feasible means for meeting the world's growing social necessities, such as energy and food production. At the same time, several (sometimes long-standing) disputes between states sharing the waters of several of the biggest world rivers awaited resolution.

The Helsinki Rules successfully and undoubtedly filled that gap. With the Helsinki Rules, the ILA offered a non-binding normative way out from the then existing deadlock of 'upper-riparian'–'lower-riparian' dualistic (exclusive) view. The solution was based on the principle of equitable and reasonable utilization, applicable in the 'international drainage basin', the most appropriate shared geographical area. An open, non-exhaustive list of factors was designed to be the framework for determining the parameters of 'equitable and reasonable utilization'. The duty of a basin state not to cause or permit significant injury to a co-basin state(s) was one factor listed in the framework of reasonable and equitable utilization. This avoided the rigidity and 'anarchy' of the Harmon Doctrine; indeed it was discarded. Such a basic position enabled the Rivers Committee to identify and formulate other pertinent rules of international water law and to elaborate on recommendations applicable to pollution of the waters of an international drainage basin. The Helsinki Rules also covered navigation on rivers and lakes that are navigable and separate or traverse the territories of two or more states, on timber floating on shared watercourses, and on the procedures for prevention and settlement of disputes.

The pressure of development needs means states depend on the use of international water resources in their territories. Faced with often lasting and uncertain situations concerning the use of those resources, these states have found in the Helsinki Rules an effective framework for resolution of existing disputes, as well as avoidance of future disputes. As such, the Helsinki Rules became accepted globally as the basis for negotiating new water treaties as well. The Helsinki Rules have also influenced the work of the International Law Commission on codification and progressive development of the law on non-navigational uses.

However, the Helsinki Rules were neither ideal nor complete. As a 'delicate balance between widely divergent views', the Helsinki Rules were subject to the scrutiny of two subsequent ILA committees. Those committees, active until 2004, studied various topics and formulated a series of articles supplementary and complementary to the Helsinki Rules with the aim of updating, upgrading and revising certain details. With approval of the Helsinki Rules in 1966, the ILA paved the way for further exhaustive study of this evolving field of international law. This eventually resulted in the comprehensive and consistent set of rules compiled in the Campione Consolidation (2000).

Ultimately, in an attempt to revise its entire body of work on international water law, the ILA approved the Berlin Rules (2004). The Berlin Rules diverge substantially from the key principles in the Helsinki Rules (1966) and all other ILA rules approved in the period 1966–2000, as well as the final output of ILC on the law of non-navigational uses of international watercourses (1996), the UN Watercourses Convention (1997), and from the ICJ judgment in the *Case concerning the Gabčikovo-Nagymaros Project* (1997). It can be argued that the substantial changes in the Berlin Rules and the attempt of their drafters to 'flow against the tide' turned out to be the cause of these sinking into oblivion.

The journey through this monograph into the history of international law in the search for the roots, evolution, and development of the international water law is no doubt worth the time and effort. This monograph comprises a rather modest historical treatise of only the first 12 years of the ILA's half-century dedication to this subject. However, besides looking back and highlighting the background of the Helsinki Rules, this monograph looks forward to broadened in-depth research into the later work of the ILA, which continued for decades after approval of the Helsinki Rules, and the benefits of such research. Such an endeavour might provide clearer and more persuasive insight into the meaning, significance, and role of the Helsinki Rules and their contribution to international water law than just the insights provided in this monograph.

One can question whether or not the fate of the Helsinki Rules is historic oblivion, or, at best, a safe pre-text for the ILA Berlin Rules or in the footnotes of theoretical discourses, or an unavoidable cornerstone of the international water law. However, one might get a satisfactory answer only after a comprehensive critical analysis and evaluation of the entire body of work by the ILA in this field of international law, including the background leading to the approval of the Berlin Rules. Such an answer would form new ground for work on the subject of international water law in our fast-changing and ever-conflictual world, indeed new ground for the work of a new generation of water lawyers. On the eve of possible new controversies between states over the use of their shared watercourses, the Helsinki Rules (particularly in the advanced, revised, and enriched form of the Campione Consolidation) may be seen as a safe pivot, marking the way out from the confusion caused by an emerging proliferation of wishful concepts and ideas aimed at coping with the rapidly changing and competing developmental needs of states sharing the same watercourse. From that perspective, for me, this study should be seen as an initial step in a new and challenging, but necessary, journey into this still young branch of international law. The Helsinki Rules will still be the rod that lights the path of researchers.

•••

To the memory of Dr. Dante A. Caponera (1921–2003) and the other members and officers of the Rivers Committee of the International Law Association for their pioneering work on international water law.

∴

Acknowledgements

I would like to extend my sincere thanks and appreciation to Dr. Salman M. A. Salman, Editor-in-Chief of *Brill Research Perspectives on International Water Law*, for suggesting the topic of the Helsinki Rules for a monograph for the journal. Earlier discussion with Dr. Salman, and his suggestions and comments on the structure and format, and also during the different stages of development of the monograph, have improved the monograph considerably.

My thanks are also extended to the anonymous external reviewers and members of the Editorial Board of the journal for their detailed and helpful comments on the monograph.

Bibliography

American Law Institute, *Restatement of the Law on Torts Second § 850A Reasonableness of the Use of Water, Annex 'Factors to Determine Reasonable Utilization', Restatement of the Law Second, Torts* (St. Paul, MN: American Law Institute Publishers, 1979).

Asian-African Legal Consultative Committee, *Report of the 11th Session* (Accra, 1970).

Asian-African Legal Consultative Committee, *Report of the 12th Session* (Colombo, 1971).

Ausness, R. C., *'The Influence of the Model Water Code on Water Resources Management Policy in Florida'*, 3:1 Journal of Land Use & Environmental Law (1987), 1–32.

Bagge, Judge A., *'Draft Proposal of Rules to be Applied by Riparian States regarding the Uses of the Water in a Drainage Basin'*, in ILA, *Report of the 51st Conference* (Tokyo, 1964), 203–214.

Baxter, R. R., *'The Nile Basin'*, in A. H. Garretson, R. D. Hayton & C. J. Olmstead (eds.), *The Law of International Drainage Basins* (Dobbs Ferry, NY: Oceana Publications, 1967), 256–297.

Berber, F. J., *'Some Methodological Considerations Concerning the Study on the Use of the Waters of International Rivers'*, printed by ILA for Rivers Committee (1957), World Bank Group Archives Disclosure Authorized, Folder ID: 1787921.

Bogdanović, S., *International Law of Water Resources: Contribution of the International Law Association (1954–2000)* (London/The Hague/Boston: Kluwer Law International, 2001).

Bourne, C., *'The International Law Association's Contribution to International Water Resources Law'*, 36 Natural Resources Journal (1996), 155–216, reprinted with an author's up-date addendum, in S. Bogdanović, *International Law of Water Resources: Contribution of the International Law Association (1954–2000)* (London/The Hague/Boston: Kluwer Law International, 2001).

Bourne, C., *International Water Law—Selected Writings of Professor Charles Bourne*, ed. by P. Wouters (London/The Hague/Boston: Kluwer Law International, 1997).

Eagleton, C., *'Diversion of Water in International Rivers: Preliminary Study Outline'*, in ILA, *Report of the 46th Conference* (Edinburg, 1954).

Economic and Social Council of the United Nations (ECOSOC), *'International Cooperation on Water Control and Utilization, Report of the UN Secretary-General under Council Resolution 346 (XII)'*, ECOSOC Doc. E/2205, 25 April 1952.

Fortuin, H., *'Report on Chapter Concerning Navigational Uses of International Rivers'*, in ILA, *Report of the 50th Conference* (Brussels, 1962), 443–469.

Garner, B. A., Ed. in Chief, *Black's Law Dictionary*, Seventh Edition (St. Paul, MN: West Group, 1999).

Hayton, R. D., *'The Formation of the Customary Rules of International Drainage Basin Law'*, in A. H. Garretson, R. D. Hayton & C. J. Olmstead (eds.), *The Law of International Drainage Basins* (Dobbs Ferry, NY: Oceana Publications, 1967), 834–895.

Inter-American Bar Association (IABA), Declaration of Buenos Aires, 19 November 1957, in IABA, *Proceedings of the Tenth Conference, Buenos Aires, 14–21 November 1957* (Buenos Aires, 1958), Vol. 1, pp. 246–248.

International Law Association (ILA), *'Dubrovnik Statement of Principles'*, in ILA, *Report of the 47th Conference* (Dubrovnik, 1956), 241–243.

ILA, *'Berlin Rules on Water Resources'*, in ILA, *Report of the 71st Conference* (Berlin, 2004).

ILA, *'Campione Consolidation of the Rules on International Water Resources, 1966–1999'*, in ILA, Report of the 69th Conference (London, 2000), 835–858.

ILA, *'Complementary Rules Applicable to International Water Resources'*, in ILA, *Report of the 62nd Conference* (Seoul, 1986), 275–292.

ILA, *'Dissenting Opinion'*, (to the Water Resources Committee Report), in ILA, *Report of the 71st Conference* (Berlin, 2004).

ILA, *'Helsinki Rules on the Uses of the Water of International Rivers'*, in ILA, *Report of the 52nd Conference* (Helsinki, 1966), 484–532.

ILA, *'Recommendation on Pollution Control'*, in ILA, *Report of the 49th Conference* (Hamburg, 1960), xviii.

ILA, *'Recommendations on the Procedures concerning the non-Navigational Uses'*, in ILA, *Report of the 49th Conference* (Hamburg, 1960), xvi–xviii.

ILA, *'Regulation of the Flow of Water of International Watercourses'*, in ILA, *Report of the 59th Conference* (Belgrade, 1980), 5–15.

ILA, *'Resolution on the Use of the Waters of International Rivers'*, in ILA, *Report of the 48th Conference* (New York, 1958), viii–x.

ILA, *'Rules on International Groundwaters'*, in ILA, *Report of the 62nd Conference* (Seoul, 1986), 251–274.

ILA, *'Rules on the Water Pollution in an International Drainage Basin'*, ILA, *Report of the 60th Conference* (Montreal, 1982).

International Law Commission (ILC), Draft Articles on the Law of Transboundary Aquifers (2008).

Kaeckenbeeck, G., *International Rivers: A Monograph Based on Diplomatic Documents* (London: Sweet and Maxwell, published for the Grotius Society, 1918).

Laylin, J. G., *'Comments Submitted to the Committee of American Branch of the ILA on "First Report of the Committee on the Uses of the Waters of International Rivers"'* (4 May 1956), printed by ILA for Rivers Committee, World Bank Archives Disclosure Authorized, Folder ID: 1787921.

Laylin, J. G., *'Principles of Law Governing the Uses of International Rivers—Contribution of the Indus Basin'* (25 April 1957), printed by ILA for Rivers Committee, World Bank Archives Disclosure Authorized, Folder ID: 1787921.

Lester, A., *'Pollution'*, in A. H. Garretson, R. D. Hayton & C. J. Olmstead (eds.), *The Law of International Drainage Basins* (Dobbs Ferry, NY: Oceana Publications, 1967), 89–123.

Lipper, J., *'Equitable Utilization'*, in A. H. Garretson, R. D. Hayton & C. J. Olmstead (eds.), *The Law of International Drainage Basins* (Dobbs Ferry, NY: Oceana Publications, 1967), 15–88.

Manner, E. J., & V. M. Mestälampi (eds.), *The Work of International Law Association on the Law of International Water Resources* (Helsinki: Finnish Branch of ILA, 1988).

McCaffrey, S., *'The Harmon Doctrine One Hundred Years Later: Buried, Not Praised'*, 36 Natural Resources Journal (1996), 549–590.

McCaffrey, S., *The Law of International Watercourses Non-Navigational Uses* (Oxford: Oxford University Press, 2001).

Muys, J. C., 'Interstate Water Compacts: The Interstate Compact and Federal-Interstate Compact', Legal Study 14, *National Water Commission* (*Report NWC-L-71-011*), (Washington, DC, 1971).

Pan American Union, *Seventh International Conference of American States, Montevideo, Uruguay, December 3, 1933, Special Handbook for the Use of Delegates*, prepared by L. S. Rowe & G. E. Borges (Baltimore, Maryland: The Sun Book & Job Printing Office, 1933).

Qadir, M., *'The Uses of the Water of International Rivers'* (27 August 1956), printed by ILA for Rivers Committee, World Bank Archives Disclosure Authorized, Folder ID: 1787921.

Ranjan, A., *'The Cauvery Water Disputes in India'*, Institute of South Asian Studies, National University of Singapore Working Paper No. 293 (2018).

Rao, K. K., *'Statement to the Indiagram'* (21 October 1958), World Bank Archives Disclosure Authorized, File ID: 1787921.

Report of a Panel of Experts, *Integrated River Basin Development*, revised edition (UN Doc. E/3066/Rev. 1), (New York: United Nations, 1970) UN Panel of Experts, 'Integrated River Basin Development' (1957, and second ed., 1970).

Salman, S. M. A., *'Entry into Force of the UN Watercourses Convention—Why should It Matter?'* 31:1 International Journal of Water Resources Development (2015), 4–16. DOI: 10.1080/07900627.2014.952072.

Salman, S. M. A., *'The Helsinki Rules, the UN Watercourse Convention and the Berlin Rules: Perspectives on International Water Law'*, 23:4 International Journal of Water Resources Development (2007), 625–640. DOI: 10.1080/07900620701488562.

Salman, S. M. A. & K. Uprety, *Conflict and Cooperation on South Asia's International Rivers: A Legal Perspective* (London/The Hague/New York: Kluwer Law International, 2002).

Sevette, P., 'Legal Aspects of Hydro-Electric Development of Rivers and Lakes of Common Interest', *UNECE Committee on Electric Power*, UN Doc. E/ECE/136, E/ECE/EP/98 Rev. 1, Geneva (1952).

Sherk, G. W., *Dividing the Waters: The Resolution of Interstate Water Conflicts in the United States* (Leiden: Brill/Nijhoff, 2000).

Sikri, S. M., *'Comments on the 1st Report of the Committee'* (22 May 1956), World Bank Archives Disclosure Authorized, Folder ID: 1787921.

Smead, E. E., *'Sic Utere Tuo Ut Alienum Non Laedes: A Basis of the State Police Power'*, 21:2 Cornell Law Review (1936), 276–292.

Smith, H. A., *The Economic Uses of International Rivers* (London: P. S. King & Son, 1933).

Tanzi, A., *The Relationship between the 1992 UNECE Convention on the Protection and Use of Transboundary Watercourses and International Lakes and the 1997 UN Convention on the Law of the Non Navigational Uses of International Watercourses: Report of the UNECE Task Force on Legal and Administrative Aspects* (Geneva, 2000).

Teclaff, L. A., & E. Teclaff, *'Bibliography on Legal and Related Aspects of the Use and Development of the Waters of International River Basins'*, in H. Garretson, R. D. Hayton & C. J. Olmstead (eds.), *The Law of International Drainage Basins* (Dobbs Ferry, NY: Oceana Publications, 1967), 609–778.

Teclaff, L. A., *The River Basin in History and Law* (The Hague: Martinus Nijhoff, 1967).

The World Bank Group, Archives Public Disclosure Authorized; *Folder: Indus Basin Dispute—International Law Association—Correspondence 01, Folder ID: 1787921*; Dates 5/1/1954–10/31/1958; Fonds: Records of the South Asia Regional Office (WB IBRD/IDA SAR); Washington, DC, 2012, Digitized: 5 August 2014.

United Nations Economic Commission for Europe, *'The First Ten Years 1947–1957'*, UN Doc. E/ECE/291 3 July 1957.

United Nations Educational, Scientific and Cultural Organization, *'The Scientific Conference on Resource Conservation and Utilization (UNSCCUR)'*, UN Doc. NS/UNR/1, 10 November 1948.

United Nations Food and Agriculture Organization (FAO), *Some General Conventions, Declarations and Resolutions adopted by Governments, International Legal Institutions and International Organizations, on the Management of International Water Resources*, compiled by Dante A. Caponera, Background Paper No. 1/Rev. 1, Legislative Branch (Rome: FAO, 1978).

United Nations General Assembly, 'Convention of the Law of the Non-Navigational Uses of International Watercourses, Report of the Sixth Committee convening as the Working Group of the Whole', UN Doc. A/51/869, 11 April 1997.

United Nations General Assembly, 'Survey of International Law in Relation to the Work of Codification of the International Law Commission', UN Doc. A/CN.4/1/Rev. 1, 10 February 1949.

United Nations Secretary-General, 'Legal problems relating to the non-navigational uses of international watercourses. Supplementary Report submitted by the Secretary-General', UN Doc. No. A/CN.4/274, 25 March 1974, reprinted in *Yearbook of the International Law Commission*, 1974, Vol. II, Part Two.

United Nations Secretary-General, 'Legal Problems Relating to the Utilization and Use of International Rivers', UN Doc. No. A/5409, 15 April 1963.

Vick, M. J., *'The Law of International Waters: Reasonable Utilization'*, 12:1 Chicago-Kent Journal of International and Comparative Law (2012), 141–178.

Zurbrügg, H., *'Report on Maintenance and Improvement of Naturally Navigable Waterways Separating or Traversing Several States'*, in ILA, *Report of the 56th Conference* (New Delhi, 1974), 117–128.

www.ingramcontent.com/pod-product-compliance
Lightning Source LLC
Chambersburg PA
CBHW031329230926
51848CB00001B/153
9789004395473